THE ESSENTIAL
VEGETARIAN
COOKBOOK

THE ESSENTIAL
VEGETARIAN
COOKBOOK

OVER 75 SAVOURY RECIPES FOR MEATLESS MEALS

CONSULTANT EDITOR
LINDA FRASER

LORENZ BOOKS
LONDON • NEW YORK • SYDNEY • BATH

This edition first published in 1995 by Lorenz Books

Lorenz Books is an imprint of
Anness Publishing Limited
Hermes House, 88-89 Blackfriars Road, London SE1 8HA

This edition is distributed in Canada by Book Express,
an imprint of Raincoast Books Distribution Limited

A CIP catalogue record for this book is available from the British Library

Publisher: Joanna Lorenz
Series Editor: Linda Fraser
Designers: Tony Paine and Roy Prescott
Photographers: Steve Baxter, Karl Adamson and Amanda Heywood
Food for Photography: Wendy Lee, Jane Stevenson, and Elizabeth Wolf Cohen
Props Stylists: Blake Minton and Kirsty Rawlings
Additional Recipes: Carla Capalbo and Laura Washburn

Printed in Singapore by Star Standard Industries Pte. Ltd.
3 5 7 9 10 8 6 4 2

ACKNOWLEDGEMENTS
For their assistance in the publication of this book
the publishers wish to thank:

Kenwood Appliances plc
New Lane
Havant
Hants
PO9 2NH

Magimix
115A High Street
Godalming
Surrey
GU7 1AQ

Prestige
Prestige House
22-26 High Street
Egham
Surrey
TW20 9DU

Le Creuset
The Kitchenware Merchants Ltd
4 Stephenson Close
East Portway, Andover
Hampshire
SP10 3RU

MEASUREMENTS
Three sets of measurements have been provided in the recipes here, in the following order:
Metric, Imperial and American. Do not mix units of measurement within each recipe.

 The apple symbol indicates a low fat, low cholesterol recipe.

CONTENTS

INTRODUCTION

Vegetarian food is increasingly popular and has come a long way from the 'brown and boring' image of ten or twenty years ago. There's a whole host of new fresh produce and exotic ingredients available nowadays and all sorts of enticing, imaginative dishes can be made with ease.

A well-balanced vegetarian diet is surprisingly easy to achieve – in fact, most vegetarians do eat a fairly healthy diet, since they consume plenty of grains, fruit, pulses and vegetables. However, vegetarians do have to be careful not to eat too many high fat products such as cheese and cream because they are potentially high cholesterol foods, and they have to watch their iron intake since iron from vegetable sources cannot be utilised by the body unless there is vitamin C present in the same meal. The simple secret is to eat a wide variety of foods and ensure that over half are starchy (or complex carbohydrate) foods.

Each day aim to eat a good selection from each of the following food groups:
• Grains such as oats and barley, pasta, rice and high fibre breakfast cereals
• Breads and potatoes
• Pulses and legumes, such as lentils, canned or dried beans and peas
• Fresh vegetables, especially leafy greens such as spinach and cabbage
• Fresh fruits

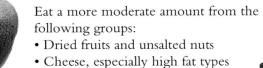

Eat a more moderate amount from the following groups:
• Dried fruits and unsalted nuts
• Cheese, especially high fat types
• Oils (use unsaturated types such as olive, sunflower, corn or peanut), margarines, butter and cream

THE VEGETARIAN STORE-CUPBOARD

Flours
A good source of protein and complex carbohydrates. Use a selection of different types, mixing wholemeal and plain flours to make pastry and bread.

Rice
Brown and wholegrain rices have more dietary fibre. Basmati and long grain are good in all sorts of dishes. Wild rice, which is not a real rice, but a type of grass has good levels of proteins.

Pulses
Although high in protein, pulses lack one of the essential amino acids. However, grain foods, although missing two different amino acids do have this one, so eaten together they make a complete protein. So when you eat pulses try to include starches in the same meal – e.g. lentils with rice, beans with pasta or humous with bread.

Pulses generally need presoaking, preferably overnight. Remember to boil them fast for the first ten minutes of cooking to destroy any mild toxins present, then lower the heat and simmer gently.

Some lentils can be cooked without presoaking – red split lentils take just 20 minutes to cook and are excellent as a thickener for soups and stews.

Beans are perfect for soups, pâtés and purées – there are lots of varieties – try butter beans, kidney beans, cannellini beans or pinto beans.

Pasta

A good source of complex carbohydrates. Quick and easy to cook, and there is a multitude of shapes and colours to add variety. Wholewheat pastas have a slightly nutty taste and chewy texture.

Potatoes

These are enjoying a renaissance at the moment, and more varieties are being grown for flavour. Choose the right variety for the method of cooking – there are often suggestions for use on the bag.

Fats and Oils

For general use choose oils high in polyunsaturates: sunflower, rape seed and groundnut oils have a very light flavour, corn and blended vegetable oils have a stronger flavour. Olive oil, which is becoming increasingly popular, is highly prized for its flavour and is also high in monosaturates which are thought to help reduce blood cholesterol levels. Fats and oils contribute vital vitamins such as A, D and E, so even if you are counting calories don't cut them out altogether.

Cheese

This is a high protein food, which is also high in calories, so for cooking, choose mature, full-flavoured cheeses – you will then not have to use as much. Many vegetarians use cheeses made from vegetarian rennet and some popular cheeses are now made this way – just be sure to check the label.

Dairy Products

There's a huge variety of dairy produce on the market; new products include créme fraîche which is a French-style soured cream (it's delicious, but, like double cream, very high in fat). Lower fat products include fromage frais, skimmed milk soft cheese, cottage and curd cheese.

Nuts and Seeds

These high protein foods are delicious in all sorts of recipes. The most popular nuts are peanuts, walnuts, almonds, cashews and pistachios. For maximum flavour, lightly roast nuts before chopping. There's an increasing range of seeds available – most useful are sunflower and sesame seeds, though poppy seeds and caraway seeds are also delicious.

Herbs

Try to use fresh herbs – either home grown, or from supermarkets and ethnic shops. Store them loosely in polythene bags in the fridge. If you do use dried herbs, buy in small amounts and replace them regularly.

Spices

Colourful, aromatic and easy to use – spices lift even the most ordinary vegetarian dishes. Spices are best roasted first to bring out the aromatic oils – easiest to do in a frying pan.

VEGETABLE PREPARATION

To enjoy their full flavour, fresh vegetables are often best prepared and served simply. These guidelines for vegetable preparation and cooking will help you make the most of seasonal bounty.

CUBING AND DICING VEGETABLES

When vegetables play a starring role in a dish, they should be cut into neat shapes such as cubes or dice. This also promotes even cooking. Cubes are generally 1.5cm/½in square, and dice are 3–6mm/⅛–¼in square.

> ### COARSE CHOPPING
> For coarsely chopped vegetables, follow the steps above, without shaving off curved sides. There is no need to cut uniform slices and strips. Alternatively, you can coarsely chop vegetables in a food processor by pulsing.

1 Peel the vegetable, if instructed. If it is long, like a carrot or celery stalk, cut it across into pieces about 7.5 cm/3in long. Lay the vegetable flat and cut it lengthways into uniform slices of the required thickness, guiding the side of the knife with your knuckles.

2 Stack the slices and cut lengthways into uniform strips of the required thickness. Gather the strips together and cut across the strips into cubes.

CHOPPING VEGETABLES

1 To chop an onion: peel it, leaving on the root end to hold the onion together. Cut in half, through the root.

2 Put one half flat on the work surface and hold the onion at the root end. Make horizontal cuts to the root but not all the way through.

3 Make vertical lengthways cuts in the onion half, again not cutting the root. Then, cut across the onion to chop it. Discard the root.

4 To chop garlic finely: set a chef's knife flat on top of the clove and bang it gently with the side of your fist to crush the garlic slightly and loosen the skin. Remove the skin.

5 Chop the garlic coarsely, then continue chopping and crushing it until it is almost a paste.

6 To chop fresh herbs: hold the leaves or sprigs together in a bunch and chop coarsely, then continue chopping until fine.

SKINNING AND SEEDING TOMATOES

Some tomatoes have tough skins and seeds. In cooking, these can become separated from the flesh and can spoil the appearance and texture of a dish. In addition, some people find tomato skins indigestible, so it is often desirable to remove them. In these cases, unless a soup, sauce or other dish is sieved before serving, it is best to skin and seed the tomatoes before using them.

If the tomatoes have tender skins and they will be eaten raw, or only briefly cooked, removing the peel is less essential. However, many people prefer to skin tomatoes for eating raw as well.

1 To skin tomatoes: cut a small cross in the skin at the base of each tomato. Immerse, three or four at a time, in boiling water. Once the cut skin begins to roll back, in about 10 seconds, lift the tomatoes out and immerse in iced water. Drain and peel.

2 To seed tomatoes: cut out the core, then cut each tomato in half across (around the 'equator'). Gently squeeze each half and shake the seeds and juice into a bowl. Scrape out any remaining seeds with the tip of a spoon or table knife.

ROASTING AND PEELING PEPPERS

There are several methods for peeling peppers, the most basic of which is shaving off the skin with a vegetable peeler. However, because peppers have awkward curves, other methods, such as roasting, are often easier. Roasting peppers also heightens the sweetness.

HANDLING CHILLIES

Do not touch eyes and lips when handling chillies, and afterwards be sure to wash your hands well.

1 Set the peppers on a rack in a grill pan and grill close to the heat. Turn the peppers to char and blister the skin all over. Alternatively, spear each pepper on a long-handled fork and hold it over a flame, turning the pepper until the skin chars.

2 Once the skin is charred, put the peppers in a plastic bag and seal it. Cool – the steam trapped inside the bag will help loosen the skin. When the peppers are cool enough to handle, peel, then cut out the stem and core.

CUTTING VEGETABLE MATCHSTICKS

These decorative shapes, also called 'julienne', are simple to cut yet look very special. Many other foods can also be cut into matchsticks, for example citrus rind, fresh root ginger, cooked meats, firm cheese and firm fruits such as apple.

For matchsticks, vegetables should be peeled and cut across into pieces about 5cm/2in long. If necessary, cut off curved sides so the vegetable has straight edges.

1 Lay each piece of vegetable flat and cut it lengthways into slices ⅛in/3mm thick or less.

2 Stack the vegetable slices and cut them lengthways into strips about ⅛in/3mm thick or less.

ROOTS AND BULBS
Carrots
Naturally sweet, carrots are used in innumerable dishes, and are tasty hot and cold, raw and cooked.

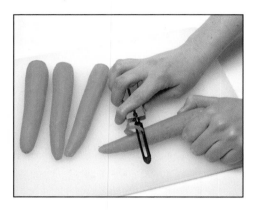

Preparation: if they are young, there is no need to peel them; just trim the ends and scrub well. Leave whole or cut as specified. If carrots have a woody core, cut it out.

Parsnips
Their sweet, nutty flavour makes a delicious addition to soups and stews or enjoy them on their own.

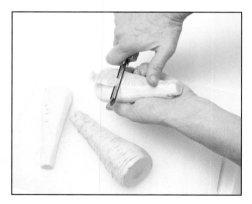

Preparation: trim the ends and peel thinly. Leave small parsnips whole; cut up larger ones. If large parsnips have a woody core, cut it out.

Turnips
Mildly piquant, turnips go well with both sweet and savoury seasonings.

Preparation: trim the ends and peel the turnips thinly.

Celeriac
The coarse knobby appearance of celeriac belies its delicate and delicious flavour.

Preparation: peel off the thick skin. Do this just before cooking because celeriac discolours when cut. If serving it raw, drop the peeled root or pieces into water acidulated with lemon juice or vinegar. Cut as instructed in recipe.

Onions
The onion is one of those ingredients basic to almost every savoury dish. They come in all sizes and shapes: pungent round onions and sweet mild onions, flat ones, large spherical Spanish ones and elongated Italian red ones. In addition, there are small pickling and button onions, shallots and spring onions.

Preparation: peel off the papery skin. Then slice, chop, etc as the recipe specifies. For spring onions, trim the root end and cut off any wilted or discoloured green leaves. Cut as specified, using just the white bulbs or both white and green parts.

Leeks
This sweet and subtle member of the onion family has myriad uses – both as a vegetable on its own and as a flavouring in soups, stews and so on.

Preparation: trim the root end and the dark green leaves. Unless the leeks are to be cooked whole, slit them open lengthways, to the centre. Wash well, then drain thoroughly. If leeks are to be sliced or chopped, do this before rinsing them thoroughly.

FRUITING VEGETABLES
Aubergines
The most familiar aubergines are the large ones with shiny purple skins, but there are also smaller purple ones and long, pale purple Chinese ones.

Preparation: trim off the stalk end. Leave aubergines whole or cut according to recipe instructions.

Courgettes
Courgettes and other thin-skinned squashes, such as pattypan, are completely edible, skin and all.

Preparation: trim the ends from courgettes. Cut as specified.

Pumpkins

Pumpkin and other squashes such as acorn and butternut, have a hard rind and central seeds and fibres that should be removed before cooking

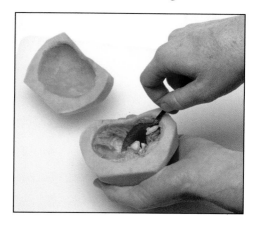

Preparation: unless baking in the skin, peel pumpkin with a large, sturdy knife. Scrape away all the seeds and stringy fibres.

LEAFY, GREEN AND OTHER VEGETABLES
Spinach

Small tender leaves have a delicate flavour and can be used raw in salads. Large, strongly flavoured, darker leaves taste better cooked.

Preparation: spinach can hide a lot of grit so needs careful rinsing. Immerse in cold water, swish round and soak for 3–4 minutes. Then lift out the spinach and immerse in fresh cold water. Repeat, then drain in a colander. Discard any damaged or yellowed leaves. Pull off tough stalks.

Green beans

Crisp green beans are available in varying sizes.

Preparation: top and tail using scissors or a knife. For older beans with strings, snap off the ends, pulling the strings from the sides as you do so. Cut large beans diagonally or shred.

Peas

Mange-touts and sugar-snap peas are completely edible. Green peas are removed from their pods for cooking.

Preparation: if green peas are in the pod, split it open and pop out the peas. Top and tail mange-touts and sugar-snap peas, pulling any tough strings from the sides as you do so.

Broccoli

Serve this green vegetable hot or leave it to cool and use in salads. It is also excellent in stir-fries.

Preparation: trim off the end of the stalk. According to recipe instructions, leave the head whole or cut off the florets, or flowers, taking a little stalk with each one.

Cauliflower

White or ivory cauliflower is the most widely available, although there are also green and purple varieties.

Preparation: cut away the large green leaves, leaving only the tiny ones if liked. Trim the stalk level with the head. Cut out the core. Leave the head whole, or break into florets before or after cooking.

Mushrooms

Cultivated button and open mushrooms are widely available; you may also find fresh wild mushrooms such as shiitake and oyster.

Preparation: rinse or wipe with damp kitchen paper (don't immerse in water as mushrooms absorb liquid readily). Trim gritty stalks, and remove tough stalks from wild mushrooms. Small mushrooms can be left whole; large ones are normally halved, quartered or sliced, or they may be diced or chopped. To stuff large mushrooms, pull off the stalks.

LIGHT LUNCHES

Vegetarian dishes for the middle of the day need to be easy to prepare and there are plenty of ideas here that will appeal to children and adults alike. Filling dishes such as Bubble and Squeak, Broccoli and Cauliflower Gratin, and Bulgur and Lentil Pilaf are good for chilly days, while in the summer Baked Polenta with Tomatoes, Ratatouille or Spaghetti with Herb Sauce are sure to please.

Eggs with Spinach and Cheese Sauce

If fresh spinach is not available, thaw 450g / 1lb frozen spinach and squeeze it hard to expel surplus liquid; use in the recipe from step 4.

INGREDIENTS

Serves 4

1kg/2lb fresh spinach, stalks removed
40g/1½oz/3 tbsp butter or margarine
45ml/3 tbsp plain flour
300ml/½ pint/1¼ cups milk
75g/3oz/¾ cup grated mature
   Cheddar cheese
pinch of English mustard powder
large pinch of freshly grated nutmeg
4 hard boiled eggs, peeled and halved
   lengthways
salt and black pepper

1 Wash but do not dry the spinach, then place in a large saucepan with just the water clinging to the leaves. Cook until the spinach is wilted and no free liquid is visible. Tip the spinach into a sieve and squeeze out as much liquid as possible, then chop the spinach.

2 Melt 25g/1oz/2 tbsp of the butter or margarine in a saucepan, stir in the flour, cook for 1 minute, then remove from the heat. Gradually add the milk, stirring constantly, then return to the heat and bring to the boil, stirring. Simmer gently for about 4 minutes.

3 Remove from the heat and stir in 50g/2oz/4 tbsp cheese, the mustard and seasoning. Preheat the grill.

4 Melt the remaining butter in a small saucepan, then stir in the spinach, nutmeg and seasoning and warm through. Transfer the spinach to a shallow baking dish and arrange the egg halves on top in a single layer.

5 Pour the sauce over the eggs, sprinkle with the remaining cheese and place under the grill until golden and bubbling.

Bubble and Squeak

The name is derived from the bubbling of the vegetables as they boiled for their first cooking, and the way they squeak when they are fried.

INGREDIENTS

Serves 4
60ml/4 tbsp butter or oil
1 onion, finely chopped
450g/1lb potatoes, cooked and mashed
225g/8oz cooked cabbage or Brussels sprouts, finely chopped
salt and black pepper

1 Heat half the butter or oil in a heavy frying pan. Add the onion and cook, stirring frequently, until softened, but not browned.

2 Mix together the potatoes, cabbage or sprouts and season to taste with salt and plenty of pepper.

3 Add the vegetables to the pan, stir well, then press the vegetable mixture into a large, even cake.

4 Cook over a moderate heat for about 15 minutes, until the cake is browned underneath.

5 Hold a large plate over the pan, then invert the vegetable cake on to it. Add the remaining butter or oil to the pan, then, when hot, slip the cake into the pan, browned side uppermost.

6 Cook the Bubble and Squeak over a moderate heat for a further 10 minutes or so, until the underside of the cake is golden brown, then serve hot, cut into wedges.

--- COOK'S TIP ---

If you don't have left-over, cooked cabbage or brussels sprouts, use fresh raw vegetables instead. Shred the cabbage first and cook both in boiling salted water until just tender. Drain thoroughly, then chop and continue from step 2.

Sweetcorn Pancakes

These crisp pancakes are delicious to serve as a snack lunch, or as a light meal with a crisp mixed salad.

Ingredients 🍎

Serves 4, makes about 12
115g/4oz/1 cup self-raising flour
1 egg white
150ml/¼ pint/⅔ cup skimmed milk
200g/7oz can sweetcorn, drained
oil, for brushing
salt and black pepper
tomato chutney, to serve

1 Place the flour, egg white, and skimmed milk in a food processor or blender with half the sweetcorn and process until smooth.

2 Season the batter well and add the remaining sweetcorn.

3 Heat a frying pan and brush with oil. Drop in tablespoons of batter and cook until set. Turn over the pancakes and cook the other side until golden. Serve hot with tomato chutney.

— Cook's Tip —
If you don't have a food processor or blender, place the milk for the batter in a large bowl and gradually beat in the egg white and milk with a wooden spoon until smooth.

Baked Polenta with Tomatoes

Ingredients 🍎

Serves 4
750ml/1¼ pints/3⅔ cups stock
175g/6oz scant 1¼ cups polenta (coarse cornmeal)
60ml/4 tbsp chopped fresh sage
5ml/1 tsp olive oil
2 beefsteak tomatoes, sliced
15ml/1 tbsp grated Parmesan cheese
salt and black pepper

1 Bring the stock to the boil in a large saucepan, then gradually stir in the polenta.

2 Continue stirring the polenta over moderate heat for about 5 minutes, until the mixture begins to come away from the sides of the pan. Stir in the chopped sage and season well, then spoon the polenta into a lightly oiled, shallow 23x33cm/9x13in tin and spread evenly. Leave to cool.

3 Preheat the oven to 200°C/400°F/ Gas 6. Cut the cooled polenta into 24 squares using a sharp knife.

4 Arrange the polenta overlapping with tomato slices in a lightly oiled, shallow ovenproof dish. Sprinkle with Parmesan and bake for 20 minutes, or until golden brown. Serve hot.

— Variation —
To make a more substantial meal, omit the Parmesan cheese and arrange slices of mozzarella cheese in between the tomato and polenta slices before baking.

Broccoli and Cauliflower Gratin

Broccoli and cauliflower make an attractive combination, and this dish is much lighter than the classic cheese sauce.

INGREDIENTS 🍎

Serves 4

1 small cauliflower (about 250g/9oz)
1 small head broccoli (about 250g/9oz)
150g/5oz/½ cup plain low fat yogurt
75g/3oz/1 cup grated low fat Cheddar cheese
5ml/1 tsp wholegrain mustard
30ml/2 tbsp wholemeal breadcrumbs
salt and black pepper

1 Break the cauliflower and broccoli into florets and cook in lightly salted, boiling water for 8–10 minutes, until just tender. Drain well and transfer to a flameproof dish.

2 Mix together the yogurt, grated cheese, and mustard, then season the mixture with pepper and spoon over the cauliflower and broccoli.

3 Sprinkle the breadcrumbs over the top and place under a grill until golden brown. Serve hot.

COOK'S TIP

When preparing the cauliflower and broccoli, discard the tougher part of the stalk, then break the florets into even-sized pieces, so they cook evenly.

Spinach and Cheese Dumplings

These little dumplings are known as *gnocchi* in Italy.

INGREDIENTS

Serves 4

175g/6oz/1¼ cups cold mashed potato
75g/3oz/½ cup semolina
115g/4oz/1 cup frozen leaf spinach,
 defrosted, squeezed and chopped
115g/4oz/½ cup ricotta cheese
25g/1oz/5 tbsp grated Parmesan cheese
30ml/2 tbsp beaten egg
2.5ml/½ tsp salt
large pinch of grated nutmeg
black pepper
30ml/2 tbsp grated Parmesan cheese
fresh basil sprigs, to garnish

For the butter

75g/3oz/6 tbsp butter
5ml/1 tsp grated lemon rind
15ml/1 tbsp lemon juice
15ml/1 tbsp chopped fresh basil

1 Place all the gnocchi ingredients except the basil in a bowl and mix well. Take small pieces of the mixture, about the size of a walnut, and roll each one back and forth a few times along the prongs of a fork until ridged. Repeat until you have 28 gnocchi and lay on a tray lined with clear film.

2 Bring a large pan of water to the boil, reduce the heat slightly, and drop the gnocchi into the simmering water. They will sink to the bottom at first, but as they cook they will rise to the surface – this will take about 2 minutes, then simmer for about 1 minute.

3 Remove the gnocchi with a slotted spoon and transfer to a lightly greased and warmed ovenproof dish.

4 Sprinkle the gnocchi with a little Parmesan cheese and grill under a high heat for about 2 minutes, or until lightly browned. Meanwhile, heat the butter in a pan and stir in the lemon rind and juice, basil and seasoning.

5 Pour a quarter of the hot butter over each portion of gnocchi and garnish with fresh basil. Serve hot.

Cheese Potato Slices

Potato slices are ideal for a quick kids' snack, or a main meal accompaniment.

INGREDIENTS

Serves 4

2 large potatoes, baked until almost cooked, then cooled
20ml/2 tbsp sunflower oil
1 garlic clove, crushed
75g/3oz/6 tbsp grated mature Cheddar cheese
salt and black pepper

1 Preheat the oven to 190°C/375°F/ Gas 5. Slice the potatoes lengthways about 1cm/½in thick and brush one side with oil. Arrange on baking sheets.

2 Mix the rest of the oil with the garlic and seasoning. Brush over the tops of the potatoes.

3 Sprinkle the cheese evenly over the potatoes and bake for about 15–20 minutes, or until the cheese topping is golden and bubbling.

--- COOK'S TIP ---

If you prefer, these potato slices can be cooked under a hot grill, or on a barbecue for 7–10 minutes.

Courgettes and Peppers au Gratin

INGREDIENTS

Serves 4

4 small courgettes, sliced
1 red pepper, seeded and sliced
1 green pepper, seeded and sliced
15ml/1 tbsp olive oil
5ml/1 tsp walnut or hazelnut oil
75ml/5 tbsp soured cream
15–30ml/1–2 tbsp milk
5ml/1 tsp grated lime rind
30ml/2 tbsp flaked almonds
salt and black pepper

1 Mix the courgettes and peppers together. Add the oils and seasoning and toss well until the vegetables are thoroughly coated in oil.

2 Preheat the oven to 180°C/350°F/ Gas 4. Blend the cream and a little milk together to give a pouring consistency. Add the lime rind and seasoning and pour evenly over the vegetables.

3 Sprinkle with the almonds and bake for 30 minutes, until the top is golden and the vegetables tender.

--- COOK'S TIP ---

To make this dish into a more substantial meal, top with a layer of sliced, cooked potatoes and a cheese sauce, in place of the soured cream and lime.

Bulgur and Lentil Pilaf

Bulgur wheat is very easy to cook and can be used in almost any way you would normally use rice, hot or cold. Some of the finer grades need hardly any cooking, so check the packet for cooking times.

INGREDIENTS 🍎

Serves 4

5ml/1 tsp olive oil
1 large onion, thinly sliced
2 garlic cloves, crushed
5ml/1 tsp ground coriander
5ml/1 tsp ground cumin
5ml/1 tsp ground turmeric
2.5ml/½ tsp ground allspice
225g/8oz/1¼ cups bulgur wheat
750ml/1¼ pints/about 3⅔ cups stock or water
115g/4oz/1½ cups button mushrooms, sliced
115g/4oz/⅔ cup green lentils
salt, black pepper and cayenne

1 Heat the oil in a non-stick saucepan and sauté the onion, garlic and spices for 1 minute, stirring.

2 Stir in the bulgur wheat and cook, stirring, for about 2 minutes, until lightly browned. Add the stock or water, mushrooms and lentils.

3 Simmer over a very low heat for about 25–30 minutes, until the bulgur wheat and lentils are tender and all the liquid is absorbed. Add more stock or water, if necessary.

4 Season well with salt, pepper and cayenne and serve hot.

COOK'S TIP

Green lentils can be cooked without pre-soaking, as they cook quite quickly and keep their shape. However, if you have the time, soaking them first will shorten the cooking time slightly.

VARIATION

To make Brown Rice and Lentil Pilaf substitute the same amount of brown rice for the bulgar wheat. You could also stir in a 300g/11oz can sweetcorn towards the end of cooking, if you like.

Potato Cakes with Goat's Cheese

INGREDIENTS

Serves 2–4

450g/1lb potatoes
10ml/2 tsp chopped fresh thyme
1 garlic clove, crushed
2 spring onions (including the green
   parts), finely chopped
30ml/2 tbsp olive oil
50g/2oz/4 tbsp unsalted butter
2 x 65g/2½oz Crottins de Chavignol
   (firm goat's cheeses)
salt and black pepper
salad leaves, such as curly endive,
   radicchio and lamb's lettuce, tossed
   in walnut dressing, to serve
thyme sprigs, to garnish

1 Peel and coarsely grate the potatoes. Using your hands squeeze out all the excess moisture, then carefully combine with the chopped thyme, garlic, spring onions and seasoning.

2 Heat half the oil and butter in a non-stick frying pan. Add two large spoonfuls of the potato mixture, spacing them well apart, and press firmly down with a spatula. Cook for 3–4 minutes on each side until golden.

3 Drain the potato cakes on kitchen paper and keep warm in a low oven. Make two more potato cakes in the same way with the remaining mixture. Meanwhile, preheat the grill.

4 Cut the cheese in half horizontally and place one half, cut side up, on each potato cake. Grill for 2–3 minutes until golden. Transfer the potato cakes to serving plates and arrange the salad leaves around them. Garnish with thyme sprigs and serve at once.

Spaghetti with Herb Sauce

Herbs make a wonderfully aromatic sauce – the heat from the pasta releases their flavour to delicious effect.

INGREDIENTS

Serves 4

50g/2oz chopped fresh mixed herbs, such as parsley, basil and thyme
2 garlic cloves, crushed
60ml/4 tbsp pine nuts, toasted
150ml/¼ pint/⅔ cup olive oil
350g/12oz dried spaghetti
60ml/4 tbsp freshly grated Parmesan cheese
salt and black pepper
basil leaves, to garnish

1 Put the herbs, garlic and half the pine nuts into a food processor. With the machine running slowly, add the oil and process to form a thick purée.

2 Cook the spaghetti in plenty of boiling salted water for 8 minutes until al dente. Drain thoroughly.

3 Transfer the herb purée to a large warm bowl, then add the spaghetti and Parmesan. Toss well to coat the pasta with the sauce. Sprinkle over the remaining pine nuts and the basil leaves and serve immediately.

Chive Omelette Stir-fry

Sesame oil has a lovely aroma and a distinctive toasted flavour. It is often added to oriental dishes at the last moment.

INGREDIENTS

Serves 3–4

2 celery sticks
2 carrots
2 small courgettes
4 spring onions
1 bunch radishes
2 eggs
15–30ml/1–2 tbsp snipped fresh chives
30ml/2 tbsp groundnut oil
1 garlic clove, chopped
1cm/½ in piece fresh root ginger, chopped
115g/4oz beansprouts
¼ head of Chinese leaves, shredded
sesame oil, to taste
salt and black pepper

1 Cut the celery, carrots, courgettes and spring onions into fine shreds. Trim the radishes, slice into rounds, then cut the rounds in half. Set aside.

2 Whisk together the eggs, chives and seasoning in a bowl. Heat about 5ml/1 tsp of the groundnut oil in an omelette pan and pour in just enough of the egg mixture to cover the base of the pan. Cook for about 1 minute until set, then turn over the omelette and cook for a further minute.

3 Tip out the omelette on to a plate and cook the rest of the egg mixture in the same way to make several omelettes, adding extra oil to the pan, if necessary. Roll up each omelette and slice thinly. Keep the omelettes warm in a low oven until required.

4 Heat the remaining oil in a wok or large frying pan, add the chopped garlic and ginger and stir-fry for a few seconds to flavour the oil.

5 Add the shredded celery, carrots and courgettes and stir-fry for 1 minute. Add the radishes, beansprouts, spring onions and Chinese leaves and stir-fry for 2–3 minutes, until the vegetables are tender but still crunchy. Sprinkle a little sesame oil over the vegetables and toss gently.

6 Serve the stir-fried vegetables at once with the sliced chive omelettes scattered over the top.

Tomato Risotto

Use plum tomatoes in this dish for their fresh vibrant flavour and firm texture.

INGREDIENTS

Serves 4

675g/1½lb firm ripe tomatoes,
  preferably plum
50g/2oz/4 tbsp butter
1 onion, finely chopped
about 1.2 litres/2 pints/5 cups
  vegetable stock
275g/10oz/1½ cups arborio rice
400g/14oz can cannellini beans,
  drained
50g/2oz Parmesan cheese, finely grated
salt and black pepper
10–12 basil leaves, shredded, and
  shavings of Parmesan cheese, to serve

1 Halve the tomatoes and scoop out the seeds into a sieve placed over a bowl. Press the seeds with a spoon to extract all the juice. Set aside.

2 Grill the tomatoes skin-side up until the skins are blackened and blistered. Rub off the skins and dice the flesh.

3 Melt the butter in a large pan, add the onion and cook for 5 minutes until beginning to soften. Add the tomatoes, the reserved juice and seasoning, then cook, stirring occasionally, for about 10 minutes.

4 Meanwhile, bring the vegetable stock to the boil in another pan.

5 Add the rice to the tomatoes and stir to coat. Add a ladleful of the stock and stir gently until absorbed. Repeat, adding a ladleful of stock at a time, until all the stock is absorbed and the rice is tender and creamy.

6 Stir in the cannellini beans and grated Parmesan and heat through for a few minutes.

7 Just before serving the risotto, sprinkle each portion with shredded basil leaves and shavings of Parmesan.

Pasta with Spring Vegetables

INGREDIENTS

Serves 4

115g/4oz broccoli florets
115g/4oz baby leeks
225g/8oz asparagus
1 small fennel bulb
115g/4oz fresh or frozen peas
40g/1½oz/3 tbsp butter
1 shallot, chopped
45ml/3 tbsp chopped fresh mixed
   herbs, such as parsley, thyme
   and sage
300ml/½ pint/1¼ cups double cream
350g/12oz dried penne pasta
salt and black pepper
freshly grated Parmesan cheese, to serve

1 Divide the broccoli florets into tiny sprigs. Cut the leeks and asparagus diagonally into 5cm/2in lengths. Trim the fennel bulb and remove any tough outer leaves. Cut into wedges, leaving the layers attached at the root ends so the pieces stay intact.

2 Cook each vegetable separately in boiling salted water until just tender – use the same water for each vegetable. Drain well and keep warm.

3 Melt the butter in a separate pan, add the chopped shallot and cook, stirring occasionally, until softened, but not browned. Stir in the herbs and cream and cook for a few minutes, until slightly thickened.

4 Meanwhile, cook the pasta in boiling salted water for 10 minutes until al dente. Drain well and add to the sauce with the vegetables. Toss gently and season with plenty of pepper.

5 Serve the pasta hot with a sprinkling of freshly grated Parmesan.

Pasta with Broccoli and Artichokes

INGREDIENTS

Serves 4

105ml/7 tbsp olive oil
1 red pepper, quartered, seeded, and
   thinly sliced
1 onion, halved and thinly sliced
5ml/1 tsp dried thyme
45ml/3 tbsp sherry vinegar
450g/1lb pasta shapes, such as penne or
   fusilli
2x175g/6oz jars marinated artichoke
   hearts, drained and thinly sliced
150g/5oz cooked broccoli, chopped
20–25 black olives, pitted
   and chopped
30ml/2 tbsp chopped fresh parsley
salt and black pepper

1 Heat 30ml/2 tbsp of the oil in a non-stick frying pan. Add the red pepper and onion and cook over low heat until just soft, 8–10 minutes, stirring occasionally.

2 Stir in the thyme, salt and vinegar. Cook for 30 seconds more, stirring, then set aside.

3 Bring a large pan of salted water to the boil. Add the pasta and cook until just tender (check package directions for timing). Drain, rinse with hot water, then drain again well. Transfer to a large bowl. Add 30ml/2 tbsp of the oil and toss well to coat.

4 Add the artichokes, broccoli, olives, parsley, onion mixture and remaining oil to the pasta. Season with salt and pepper. Stir to blend. Leave to stand at least 1 hour before serving, or chill overnight.

Onion and Thyme Tart

INGREDIENTS

Serves 6

30ml/2 tbsp butter or olive oil
2 onions, thinly sliced
2.5ml/½ tsp fresh or dried thyme
1 egg
120ml/4fl oz/½ cup soured cream or
   natural yogurt
10ml/2 tsp poppy seeds
large pinch of ground mace or nutmeg
salt and black pepper

For the base

115g/4oz/1cup plain flour
6.5ml/1¼ tsp baking powder
2.5ml/½ tsp salt
40g/1½oz/3 tbsp cold butter
90ml/6 tbsp milk

1 Heat the butter or oil in a medi-um-size frying pan. Add the onions and cook over low heat for 10–12 minutes, until soft and golden. Season with thyme, salt and pepper. Remove from the heat and let cool. Preheat the oven to 220°C/425°F/Gas 7.

2 For the base, sift the flour, baking powder, and salt into a bowl. Using a pastry blender or two knives, cut the butter into the dry ingredients until the mixture resembles breadcrumbs. Add the milk and stir in lightly with a wooden spoon to make a dough.

3 Turn out the dough onto a floured surface and knead lightly.

4 Pat out the dough into a 20cm/8in round. Transfer to a deep 20cm/8in baking tin. Press the dough into an even layer then cover the dough evenly with the onions.

5 Beat together the egg and soured cream or yogurt. Spread evenly over the onions. Sprinkle with the poppy seeds and mace or nutmeg. Bake for about 25–30 minutes until the egg topping is puffed and golden.

6 Leave the tart to cool in the pan for 10 minutes. Slip a knife between the tart and the tin to loosen, then unmould onto a plate. Cut the tart into wedges and serve warm.

Leek and Courgette Bake

This creamy vegetable dish is lovely for a light lunch; add mushrooms, peppers or sweetcorn, if you like.

INGREDIENTS

Serves 4

40g/1½oz/3 tbsp butter
1 leek, finely chopped
2 large or 4 medium courgettes, trimmed and coarsely grated
30ml/2 tbsp plain flour
150ml/¼ pint/⅔ cup milk
5ml/1 tsp made English mustard
15ml/1 tbsp fromage frais
10ml/2 tsp chopped fresh basil
5ml/1 tsp caraway seeds (optional)
3 eggs, separated
salt and black pepper

1 Melt the butter in a medium to large pan, add the leek and cook for 2 minutes, stirring. Add the courgettes and flour and cook for a further 2 minutes, stirring.

2 Gradually stir in the milk, then bring to the boil, stirring to make sure there are no lumps, and cook for 2 minutes. Remove from the heat.

3 Season with salt, pepper and mustard, stir in the fromage frais, basil and caraway seeds, if using. Beat in the egg yolks. Preheat the oven to 190°C/375°F/Gas 5.

4 Whisk the egg whites until they form stiff peaks. Using a metal spoon, carefully fold the egg whites into the courgette mixture.

5 Spoon into a 1.75 litre/3 pint casserole or ovenproof dish. Bake for 30–35 minutes, until well risen and golden brown. Serve immediately.

Ratatouille

INGREDIENTS

Serves 4

2 large aubergines, roughly chopped
4 courgettes, roughly chopped
150ml/¼ pint/⅔ cup olive oil
2 onions, sliced
2 garlic cloves, chopped
1 large red pepper, seeded and roughly
  chopped
2 large yellow peppers, seeded and
  roughly chopped
fresh rosemary sprig
fresh thyme sprig
5ml/1 tsp coriander seeds, crushed
3 plum tomatoes, skinned, seeded and
  chopped
8 basil leaves, torn
salt and black pepper
fresh parsley or basil sprigs,
  to garnish

1 Sprinkle the aubergines and courgettes with salt, then put them in a
colander with a plate and weight on top
to extract the bitter juices. Leave for
about 30 minutes.

2 Heat the olive oil in a large
saucepan. Add the onions, fry
gently for about 6–7 minutes, until just
softened, then add the garlic and cook
for another 2 minutes.

3 Rinse the aubergines and courgettes
and pat dry with kitchen paper. Add
to the pan with the peppers, increase
the heat and sauté until the peppers are
just turning brown.

4 Add the herbs and coriander seeds,
then cover the pan and cook gently
for about 40 minutes.

5 Add the tomatoes and season well.
Cook gently for a further 10 minutes, until the vegetables are soft but
not too mushy. Remove the sprigs of
herbs. Stir in the torn basil leaves and
check the seasoning. Leave to cool
slightly and serve warm or cold, garnished with sprigs of parsley or basil.

MID-WEEK MEALS

There are myriad vegetarian recipes with a summery Mediterranean flavour which make delicious meals whether you are cooking for family or friends. Choose from excellent traditional dishes, such as Middle-Eastern Vegetable Stew, and Sweetcorn and Bean Tamale Pie. Or try one of the delicious and enticing contemporary ideas, such as Baked Squash with Parmesan or Spinach and Hazelnut Lasagne.

Spinach and Hazelnut Lasagne

A vegetarian dish that is hearty enough to satisfy meat-eaters too. Use frozen spinach if you're short of time.

INGREDIENTS 🍎

Serves 4

900g/2lb fresh spinach
300ml/½ pint/1¼ cups vegetable stock
1 medium onion, finely chopped
1 garlic clove, crushed
75g/3oz/¾ cup hazelnuts
30ml/2 tbsp chopped fresh basil
6 lasagne sheets
400g/14oz can chopped tomatoes
200g/7oz/1 cup low fat fromage frais
slivered hazelnuts and chopped parsley, to garnish

1 Preheat the oven to 200°C/400°F/ Gas 6. Wash the spinach and place in a pan with just the water that clings to the leaves. Cook the spinach over a fairly high heat for 2 minutes until wilted. Drain well.

2 Heat 30ml/2 tbsp of the stock in a large pan and simmer the onion and garlic until soft. Stir in the spinach, hazelnuts and basil.

3 In a large ovenproof dish, layer the spinach, lasagne, and tomatoes. Season well between the layers. Pour over the remaining stock. Spread the fromage frais over the top.

4 Bake the lasagne for about 45 minutes, or until golden brown. Serve hot, sprinkled with lines of slivered hazelnuts and chopped parsley.

--- COOK'S TIP ---

The flavour of hazelnuts is improved by roasting. Place them on a baking sheet and bake in a moderate oven, or under a hot grill, until light golden.

Broccoli and Ricotta Cannelloni

INGREDIENTS

Serves 4

12 dried cannelloni tubes, 7.5cm/
  3in long
450g/1lb/4 cups broccoli florets
75g/3oz/1½ cups fresh breadcrumbs
150ml/¼ pint/⅔ cup milk
60ml/4 tbsp olive oil, plus extra for
  brushing
225g/8oz/1 cup ricotta cheese
pinch of grated nutmeg
90ml/6 tbsp grated Parmesan or
  Pecorino cheese
salt and black pepper
30ml/2 tbsp pine nuts, for sprinkling

For the tomato sauce

30ml/2 tbsp olive oil
1 onion, finely chopped
1 garlic clove, crushed
2 x 400g/14oz cans chopped tomatoes
15ml/1 tbsp tomato purée
4 black olives, stoned and chopped
5ml/1 tsp dried thyme

1 Preheat the oven to 190°C/375°F/ Gas 5 and lightly grease an oven-proof dish with olive oil. Bring a large saucepan of water to the boil, add a little olive oil and simmer the cannelloni, uncovered, for about 6–7 minutes, or until nearly cooked.

2 Meanwhile, steam or boil the broccoli for 10 minutes, until tender. Drain the pasta, rinse under cold water and reserve. Drain the broccoli and leave to cool, then place in a food processor or blender, whizz until smooth and set aside.

3 Place the breadcrumbs in a bowl, add the milk and oil and stir until softened. Add the ricotta, broccoli purée, nutmeg, 60ml/4 tbsp of the Parmesan cheese and seasoning, then set aside.

4 To make the sauce, heat the oil in a frying pan and add the onions and garlic. Fry for 5–6 minutes, until softened, then stir in the tomatoes, tomato purée, black olives, thyme and seasoning. Boil rapidly for 2–3 minutes, then pour into the base of the dish.

5 Spoon the cheese mixture into a piping bag fitted with a 1cm/½in nozzle. Carefully open the cannelloni tubes. Standing each one upright on a board, pipe the filling into each tube. Lay them in rows in the tomato sauce.

6 Brush the tops of the cannelloni with a little olive oil and sprinkle over the remaining Parmesan cheese and pine nuts. Bake in the oven for about 25–30 minutes, until golden on top.

Macaroni Cheese with Leeks

Leeks add a new twist and extra flavour to an ever-popular family favourite.

INGREDIENTS

Serves 4
175g/6oz/1½ cups short-cut
   macaroni
50g/2oz/4 tbsp butter
4 leeks, chopped
60ml/4 tbsp plain flour
750ml/1¼ pints/3 cups milk
200g/7oz/scant 2 cups grated mature
   Cheddar cheese
45ml/3 tbsp fresh breadcrumbs
salt and black pepper

--- COOK'S TIP ---

The sauce can be flavoured with mustard or chopped herbs, such as parsley, chives or thyme.

1 Preheat the oven to 200°C/400°F/ Gas 6. Cook the macaroni in plenty of boiling salted water for 8–10 minutes, until tender. Drain well.

2 Melt the butter in a saucepan, add the leeks and cook, stirring occasionally, for about 4 minutes. Stir in the flour, cook for 1 minute, then remove the pan from the heat.

3 Gradually stir the milk into the pan, then return to the heat and bring to the boil, stirring. Simmer for about 3 minutes.

4 Remove from the heat and stir in the macaroni and most of the cheese, and season to taste. Pour the macaroni mixture into a baking dish. Mix together the breadcrumbs and the remaining cheese, then sprinkle over the dish. Bake for 20 – 25 minutes, until the topping is golden.

Broccoli and Stilton Puff

Cauliflower can be used instead of broccoli in this dish, or if you like, you can use a mixture of the two .

INGREDIENTS

Serves 4
675g/1½lb broccoli
4 eggs, separated
115g/4oz blue Stilton cheese,
   crumbled
about 10ml/2 tsp wholegrain or
   French mustard
salt and black pepper

1 Preheat the oven to 190°C/375°F/ Gas 5. Thoroughly butter a 19cm/7½ in soufflé dish.

2 Cook the broccoli in boiling salted water until just tender. Drain the broccoli, refresh under cold running water, then drain well.

3 Place the broccoli in a food processor with the egg yolks and process until smooth. Tip the mixture into a bowl then mix in the Stilton and add mustard and seasoning to taste.

4 Whisk the egg whites until stiff but not dry, then gently fold into the broccoli mixture in three batches. Transfer the broccoli mixture to the dish and bake for about 35 minutes, until risen, just set in the centre, and golden. Serve immediately.

Sweetcorn and Bean Tamale Pie

INGREDIENTS

Serves 4

2 corn cobs
30ml/2 tbsp vegetable oil
1 onion, chopped
2 garlic cloves, crushed
1 red pepper, seeded and chopped
2 green chillies, seeded and chopped
10ml/2 tsp ground cumin
450g/1lb ripe tomatoes, peeled, seeded
   and chopped
15ml/1 tbsp tomato purée
425g/15oz can red kidney beans,
   drained and rinsed
15ml/1 tbsp chopped fresh oregano
oregano leaves, to garnish

For the topping

115g/4oz/1 cup polenta
15ml/1 tbsp plain flour
2.5ml/½ tsp salt
10ml/2 tsp baking powder
1 egg, lightly beaten
100ml/3½fl oz/½ cup milk
15ml/1 tbsp butter, melted
50g/2oz smoked Cheddar cheese,
   grated

1 Preheat the oven to 220°C/425°F/Gas 7. Remove the outer husks and silky threads from the corn cobs, then par-boil in boiling, but not salted, water for 8 minutes. Drain and leave until cool enough to handle, then run a sharp knife down the corn cobs to remove the kernels.

2 Heat the oil in a large pan and fry the onion, garlic and pepper for 5 minutes, until softened. Add the chillies and cumin and fry for 1 minute.

3 Stir in the tomatoes, tomato purée, beans, corn kernels and oregano. Season. Bring to the boil, then simmer, uncovered, for 10 minutes.

4 Meanwhile, make the topping. Mix together the polenta, flour, salt, baking powder, egg, milk and butter in a bowl to form a smooth, thick batter.

5 Transfer the corn kernels and beans to an ovenproof dish, spoon the polenta mixture over the top and spread evenly. Bake for 30 minutes. Remove from the oven, sprinkle over the cheese, then return to the oven for a further 5–10 minutes, until golden.

Vegetable Chilli

INGREDIENTS

Serves 8

50ml/2fl oz/¼ cup olive or vegetable oil
2 onions, chopped
75g/3oz finely sliced celery
2 carrots, cut in 1cm/½in cubes
2 garlic cloves, crushed
2.5ml/½ tsp celery seeds
1.25ml/¼ tsp cayenne
5ml/1 tsp ground cumin
45ml/3 tbsp chilli powder
425g/15oz canned chopped plum
   tomatoes with their juice
250ml/8fl oz/1 cup vegetable stock
   or water
2.5ml/½ tsp fresh or dried thyme
1 bay leaf
350g/12oz cauliflower florets
3 courgettes cut in 1cm/½in cubes
300g/11oz can sweetcorn, drained
425g/15oz can kidney or pinto beans,
   drained
hot pepper sauce (optional)
salt

1 Heat the oil in a large flameproof
casserole or heavy saucepan and
add the onions, celery, carrots, and
garlic. Cover the casserole and cook
over a low heat for 8–10 minutes
stirring from time to time, until the
onions are softened.

2 Stir in the celery seeds, cayenne,
cumin, and chilli powder. Mix
well. Add the tomatoes, stock or water,
salt, thyme and bay leaf. Stir. Cook for
15 minutes, uncovered.

3 Add the cauliflower, courgettes
and sweetcorn. Cover and cook
for a further 15 minutes.

4 Add the kidney or pinto beans, stir
well, and cook for 10 minutes
more, uncovered. Check the seasoning, and add a dash of hot pepper sauce
if desired. Good with freshly boiled
rice or baked potatoes.

Vegetable Ribbons

This may just tempt a few fussy eaters to eat up!

INGREDIENTS

Serves 4
3 medium carrots
3 medium courgettes
120ml/4fl oz/½ cup vegetable stock
30ml/2 tbsp chopped fresh parsley
salt and black pepper

1 Using a vegetable peeler or sharp knife, cut the carrots and courgettes into thin ribbons.

2 Bring the stock to a boil in a large saucepan and add the carrots. Return the stock to a boil, then add the courgettes. Boil rapidly for 2–3 minutes, or until the vegetable ribbons are just tender.

3 Stir in the parsley, season lightly, and serve hot.

— COOK'S TIP —

In the summer, when fresh herbs are readily available, try chopped thyme or snipped chives in place of the parsley, or use a mixture of all three.

Veggie Burgers

INGREDIENTS

Serves 4
115g/4oz cup mushrooms, finely chopped
1 small onion, chopped
1 small courgette, chopped
1 carrot, chopped
25g/1oz unsalted peanuts or cashews
115g/4oz/2 cups fresh bread crumbs
30ml/2 tbsp chopped fresh parsley
5ml/1 tsp yeast extract
salt and black pepper
fine oatmeal or flour, for shaping

1 Cook the mushrooms in a non-stick pan without oil, stirring, for 8–10 minutes to remove all the moisture.

2 Process the onion, courgette, carrot, and nuts in a food processor until beginning to bind together.

3 Stir in the mushrooms, bread-crumbs, parsley, yeast extract, and seasoning to taste. With the oatmeal or flour, shape into four burgers. Chill.

4 Cook the burgers in a non-stick frying pan with very little oil or under a hot grill for 8–10 minutes, turning once, until the burgers are cooked and golden brown. Serve hot with a crisp salad.

— COOK'S TIP —

You can prepare these burgers up to a day before cooking. Arrange them on a plate or tray and cover with cling film, then chill until ready to cook.

Aubergine Lasagne

INGREDIENTS

Serves 4

3 medium aubergines, sliced
75ml/5 tbsp olive oil
2 large onions, finely chopped
2 x 400g/14oz cans chopped tomatoes
5ml/1 tsp dried mixed herbs
2–3 garlic cloves, crushed
6 sheets no pre-cook lasagne
salt and black pepper

For the cheese sauce

25g/1oz/2 tbsp butter
25g/1oz/2 tbsp plain flour
300ml/½ pint/1¼ cups milk
2.5ml/½ tsp mustard
115g/4oz/8 tbsp grated mature
    Cheddar
15g/½oz /1 tbsp grated Parmesan
    cheese

1 Layer the sliced aubergine in a colander, sprinkling lightly with salt between each layer. Leave to stand for 1 hour, then rinse and pat dry.

2 Heat 60ml/4 tbsp oil in a large pan, fry the aubergine and drain on kitchen paper. Add the remaining oil to the pan, cook the onions for 5 minutes, then stir in the tomatoes, herbs, garlic and seasoning. Bring to the boil and simmer, covered for 30 minutes.

3 Meanwhile, make the cheese sauce; melt the butter in a pan, stir in the flour and cook gently for 1 minute, stirring. Gradually stir in the milk. Bring to the boil, stirring, and cook for 2 minutes. Remove from the heat and stir in the mustard, cheeses and seasoning.

4 Preheat the oven to 200°C/400°F/ Gas 6. Arrange half the aubergines in the base of an ovenproof dish, spoon over half the tomato sauce. Arrange three sheets of lasagne on top. Repeat with a second layer.

5 Spoon over the cheese sauce, cover and bake for 30 minutes. Remove the lid for the last 10 minutes to brown the crust. Serve hot with a mixed salad.

FREEZER NOTE

This dish freezes well; cook for only 20 minutes, cool, then freeze. Reheat at 170°C/375°F/Gas 3 for 20 minutes; increase the temperature to 200°C/400°F/ Gas 6 for 10 minutes to brown the top.

Calzone

INGREDIENTS 🍎

Makes 4

450g/1lb/4 cups plain flour
pinch of salt
1 sachet easy blend yeast
about 350ml/12fl oz/1½ cups warm
    water

For the filling

5ml/1 tsp olive oil
1 medium red onion, thinly sliced
3 medium courgettes, about 350g/12oz
    total weight, sliced
2 large tomatoes, diced
150g/5oz mozzarella cheese, diced
15ml/1 tbsp chopped fresh oregano
skimmed milk, to glaze
salt and black pepper

1 To make the dough, sift the flour and salt into a bowl and stir in the yeast. Stir in just enough warm water to mix to a soft dough.

2 Knead for 5 minutes until smooth. Cover and leave in a warm place for about 1 hour, or until doubled in size.

3 Meanwhile, to make the filling, heat the oil and sauté the onion and courgettes for 3–4 minutes. Remove from the heat and add the tomatoes, cheese, oregano and seasoning.

4 Preheat the oven to 220°C/425°F/ Gas 7. Knead the dough lightly and divide into four. Roll out each piece on a lightly floured surface to a 20cm/8in round, and place a quarter of the filling on one half.

5 Brush the edges with milk and fold over to enclose the filling. Press firmly to enclose. Brush with milk.

6 Bake on an oiled baking sheet for 15–20 minutes. Serve hot or cold.

—— COOK'S TIP ——
Don't add too much water to the dough when mixing otherwise the dough will be difficult to roll out – it should be soft, but not at all sticky.

Pasta with Chick-pea Sauce

INGREDIENTS 🍎

Serves 4

300g/10oz/2 cups pasta
5ml/1 tsp olive oil
1 small onion, finely chopped
1 garlic clove, crushed
1 celery stick, finely chopped
425g/15oz can chick-peas, drained
250ml/8fl oz/1 cup passata
salt and black pepper
chopped fresh parsley, to garnish

1 Heat the olive oil in a non-stick pan and sauté the onion, garlic, and celery until softened, not browned. Stir in the chick-peas and tomato sauce, then cover and simmer for 15 minutes.

2 Cook the pasta in a large pan of boiling, lightly salted water until just tender. Drain the pasta and toss into the sauce, then season to taste with salt and pepper. Sprinkle with chopped fresh parsley, then serve hot.

VARIATION

To make Pasta with Beans, omit the chick-peas and substitute a 425g/15oz can of mixed beans, or use the same size can of kidney beans instead.

Pepperonata Pizza

INGREDIENTS 🍎

Makes 2 large pizzas

450g/1lb/4 cups plain flour
pinch of salt
1 sachet easy blend yeast
about 350ml/12fl oz/1½ cups warm
    water

For the topping

1 onion, sliced
10ml/2 tsp olive oil
2 large red and 2 yellow peppers,
    seeded and sliced
1 garlic clove, crushed
400g/14oz can tomatoes
8 pitted black olives, halved
salt and black pepper

COOK'S TIP

In the summer when there are plenty of fresh tomatoes around, use about 350g/12oz in place of the canned tomatoes. Dip them into boiling water for 30 seconds to remove the skins, then chop them roughly.

1 To make the dough, sift the flour and salt into a bowl and stir in the yeast. Stir in just enough warm water to mix to a soft dough.

2 Knead for 5 minutes until smooth. Cover and leave in a warm place for about 1 hour, or until doubled in size.

3 To make the topping, sauté the onion in the oil until soft, then stir in the peppers, garlic and tomatoes. Cover and simmer for 30 minutes, until no liquid remains. Season to taste.

4 Preheat the oven to 220°C/450°F/ Gas 8. Divide the dough in half and press out each piece on a lightly oiled baking sheet to a 28cm/11in round, turning up the edges slightly.

5 Spread over the topping, dot with olives, and bake for 15–20 minutes. Serve hot or cold, with salad.

Middle-Eastern Vegetable Stew

A spiced dish of mixed vegetables makes a delicious and filling vegetarian main course. Children may prefer less chilli.

INGREDIENTS

Serves 4–6
45ml/3 tbsp vegetable stock
1 green pepper, seeded and sliced
2 medium courgettes, sliced
2 medium carrots, sliced
2 celery sticks, sliced
2 medium potatoes, diced
400g/14oz can chopped tomatoes
5ml/1 tsp chilli powder
30ml/2 tbsp chopped fresh mint
15ml/1 tbsp ground cumin
400g/14oz can chick-peas, drained
salt and black pepper
mint sprigs, to garnish

1 Heat the vegetable stock in a large flameproof casserole until boiling, then add the sliced pepper, courgettes, carrots, and celery. Stir over high heat for 2–3 minutes, until the vegetables are just beginning to soften.

2 Add the potatoes, tomatoes, chilli powder, mint, and cumin. Add the chick-peas and bring to the boil.

3 Reduce the heat, cover the casserole, and simmer for 30 minutes, or until all the vegetables are tender. Season to taste with salt and pepper and serve hot, garnished with mint leaves.

—— COOK'S TIP ——
Chick-peas are traditional in this type of Middle-Eastern dish, but if you prefer, red kidney beans or navy beans can be used instead.

—— VARIATION ——
Other vegetables can be substituted for those in the recipe, just use whatever you have to hand – try swede, sweet potato or parsnips.

Summer Vegetable Braise

Tender, young vegetables are ideal for quick cooking in a minimum of liquid. Use any mixture of the family's favourite vegetables, as long as they are of similar size.

INGREDIENTS

Serves 4
175g/6oz/2½ cups baby carrots
175g/6oz/2 cups sugar-snap peas or mange-tout
115g/4oz/1¼ cups baby corn
90ml/6 tbsp vegetable stock
10ml/2 tsp lime juice
salt and black pepper
chopped fresh parsley and snipped fresh chives, to garnish

1 Place the carrots, peas, and baby corn in a large heavy-based saucepan with the vegetable stock and lime juice. Bring to the boil.

2 Cover the pan and reduce the heat, then simmer for 6–8 minutes, shaking the pan occasionally, until the vegetables are just tender.

3 Season the vegetables to taste with salt and pepper, then stir in the chopped fresh parsley and snipped fresh chives. Cook the vegetables for a few seconds more, stirring them once or twice until the herbs are well mixed, then serve at once.

— COOK'S TIP —
You can make this dish in the winter too, but cut larger, tougher vegetables into chunks and cook for slightly longer.

— VARIATION —
To make a more substantial dish, tip the cooked vegetables into a gratin dish and scatter with a mixture of grated cheese and breadcrumbs and grill until golden and bubbling.

Cauliflower with Three Cheeses

The flavour of three cheeses gives a new twist to cauliflower cheese.

INGREDIENTS

Serves 4
4 baby cauliflowers
250ml/8fl oz/1 cup single cream
75g/3oz dolcelatte cheese, diced
75g/3oz mozzarella cheese, diced
45ml/3 tbsp freshly grated Parmesan
   cheese
freshly grated nutmeg
black pepper
toasted breadcrumbs, to garnish

COOK'S TIP

If little baby cauliflowers are not available, you could use one large cauliflower. Divide into quarters and then remove the central core.

---

1 Cook the cauliflowers in a large pan of boiling salted water for 8–10 minutes, until just tender.

2 Meanwhile, put the cream into a small pan with the cheeses. Heat gently until the cheeses have melted, stirring occasionally. Season with nutmeg and freshly ground pepper.

3 When the cauliflowers are cooked, drain them thoroughly and place one on each of four warmed plates.

4 Spoon a little of the cheese sauce over each cauliflower and sprinkle each with a few of the toasted bread-crumbs. Serve at once.

Winter Vegetable Hot-pot

Use whatever vegetables you have to hand in this richly flavoured and substantial one-pot meal.

INGREDIENTS

Serves 4
2 onions, sliced
4 carrots, sliced
1 small swede, sliced
2 parsnips, sliced
3 small turnips, sliced
½ celeriac, cut into matchsticks
2 leeks, thinly sliced
1 garlic clove, chopped
1 bay leaf, crumbled
30ml/2 tbsp chopped fresh mixed
   herbs, such as parsley and thyme
300ml/½ pint/1¼ cups vegetable stock
15ml/1 tbsp plain flour
675g/1½ lb red-skinned potatoes,
   scrubbed and thinly sliced
50g/2oz/4 tbsp butter
salt and black pepper

1 Preheat the oven to 190°C/375°F/ Gas 5. Arrange all the vegetables, except the potatoes, in layers in a large casserole with a tight-fitting lid.

2 Season the vegetable layers lightly with salt and pepper and sprinkle them with garlic, crumbled bay leaf and chopped herbs as you go.

3 Blend the stock into the flour and pour over the vegetables. Arrange the potatoes in overlapping layers on top. Dot with butter and cover tightly.

4 Cook in the oven for 1¼ hours, or until the vegetables are tender. Remove the lid from the casserole and cook for a further 15–20 minutes until the top layer of potatoes is golden and crisp at the edges. Serve hot.

Baked Squash with Parmesan

Spaghetti squash is an unusual vegetable – the flesh separates into long strands when baked. One squash makes an excellent supper dish for two.

INGREDIENTS

Serves 2

1 medium spaghetti squash
115g/4oz/½ cup butter
45ml/3 tbsp chopped mixed fresh
    herbs, such as parsley, chives
    and oregano
1 garlic clove, crushed
1 shallot, chopped
5ml/1 tsp lemon juice
50g/2oz/½ cup freshly grated
    Parmesan cheese
salt and black pepper

1 Preheat the oven to 180°C/350°F/ Gas 4. Cut the squash in half lengthways. Place the halves, cut side down, in a roasting tin. Pour a little water around them, then bake for about 40 minutes, until tender.

2 Meanwhile, put the butter, herbs, garlic, shallot and lemon juice in a food processor and process until thoroughly blended and creamy in consistency. Season to taste.

3 When the squash is tender, scrape out any seeds and cut a thin slice from the base of each half, so that they will sit level. Place the squash halves on warmed serving plates.

4 Using a fork, pull out a few of the spaghetti-like strands in the centre of each. Add a dollop of herb butter, then sprinkle with a little of the grated Parmesan. Serve the remaining herb butter and Parmesan separately, adding them as you pull out more strands.

Borlotti Beans with Mushrooms

A mixture of wild and cultivated mushrooms helps to give this dish a rich and nutty flavour.

INGREDIENTS

Serves 4

30ml/2 tbsp olive oil
50g/2oz/4 tbsp butter
2 shallots, chopped
2–3 garlic cloves, crushed
675g/1½lb mixed mushrooms,
  thickly sliced
4 pieces sun-dried tomatoes in oil,
  drained and chopped
90ml/6 tbsp dry white wine
400g/14oz can borlotti beans
45ml/3 tbsp grated Parmesan cheese
30ml/2 tbsp chopped fresh parsley
salt and black pepper
freshly cooked pappardelle pasta,
  to serve

1 Heat the oil and butter in a frying pan and fry the shallots until soft.

2 Add the garlic and mushrooms to the pan and fry for 3–4 minutes. Stir in the sun-dried tomatoes, wine and seasoning to taste.

3 Stir in the borlotti beans and cook for 5–6 minutes, until most of the liquid has evaporated and the beans are warmed through.

4 Stir in the grated Parmesan cheese. Sprinkle with parsley and serve immediately with pappardelle.

Root Vegetable Couscous

Cheap and plentiful, autumn's crop of flavourful root vegetables is perfect for this delicious vegetarian main course. The spiced red sauce is fairly fiery and is not for the faint hearted! If you prefer your food less hot, leave out the harissa.

INGREDIENTS

Serves 4

350g/12oz/2 cups couscous
45ml/3 tbsp olive oil
4 baby onions, halved
675g/1½lb mixed root vegetables, such as parsnips, carrots, swede, turnip, celeriac and sweet potatoes, cut into chunks
2 garlic cloves, crushed
pinch of saffron strands
2.5ml/½ tsp ground cinnamon
2.5ml/½ tsp ground ginger
2.5ml/½ tsp ground turmeric
5ml/1 tsp ground cumin
5ml/1 tsp ground coriander
15ml/1 tbsp tomato purée
450ml/¾ pint/1⅞ cups hot vegetable stock
1 small fennel bulb, quartered
115g/4oz/1 cup cooked or canned chick-peas
50g/2oz/⅓ cup seedless raisins
30ml/2 tbsp chopped fresh coriander
30ml/2 tbsp chopped fresh flat leaf parsley
salt and black pepper

For the spiced red sauce

15ml/1 tbsp olive oil
15ml/1 tbsp lemon juice
15ml/1 tbsp chopped fresh coriander
2.5–5ml/½–1 tsp harissa

1 Put the couscous in a bowl, cover with hot water and drain. Spread out on to a tray and leave for about 20 minutes, sprinkling over a little water every 5 minutes to keep the couscous grains moist.

2 Meanwhile, heat the oil in a large frying pan and fry the onions for about 3 minutes. Add the mixed root vegetables and fry gently for about 5 minutes, until softened.

3 Add the garlic and spices to the frying pan and cook for 1 minute, stirring. Transfer the vegetable mixture to a large deep saucepan.

4 Stir the tomato purée and stock into the vegetable mixture, then add the fennel, chick-peas, raisins, chopped fresh coriander and flat leaf parsley. Bring to the boil.

5 Fork the couscous to break up any lumps and put into a steamer lined with muslin and place the steamer over the vegetable mixture.

6 Cover the steamer with a lid or foil and simmer for 15–20 minutes, until the vegetables are tender and the couscous is piping hot.

7 To make the spiced red sauce, strain about 250ml/8fl oz/1 cup of the liquid from the vegetables into a small pan. Stir in the olive oil, lemon juice, coriander and harissa, to taste.

8 Spoon the couscous on to a serving plate and pile the vegetables on top. Serve at once, handing round the spiced red sauce separately.

--- COOK'S TIP ---

Harissa is a very fiery Tunisian chilli sauce. It can be bought ready-made in small cans from Middle-Eastern shops.

DINNER PARTY DISHES

There are plenty of vegetarian dishes that are colourful, flavoursome and sure to impress. Try a delicious and filling dish such as Golden Vegetable Paella or Asparagus and Cheese Risotto – both are excellent choices for a main course. If you prefer, some of the lighter dishes, such as Goat's Cheese Salad, can be served either as a starter, or doubled up to make enough for a main meal.

Greek Spinach and Cheese Pies

INGREDIENTS

Makes 4

15ml/1 tbsp olive oil
1 small onion, finely chopped
275g/10oz fresh spinach, stalks removed
50g/2oz/4 tbsp butter, melted
4 sheets of filo pastry (about 45 x 25cm/18 x 10in)
1 egg
a good pinch of grated nutmeg
75g/3oz/¾ cup crumbled feta cheese
15ml/1 tbsp grated Parmesan cheese
salt and black pepper

1 Preheat the oven to 190°C/375°F/ Gas 5. Heat the oil in a pan, add the onion and fry gently for 5–6 minutes, until softened.

2 Add the spinach leaves and cook, stirring, until the spinach has wilted and some of the liquid evaporated. Leave to cool.

3 Brush four 10cm/4in diameter loose-based tartlet tins with a little melted butter. Take two sheets of the filo pastry and cut each into eight 11cm/4½in squares. Keep the remaining sheets covered.

4 Brush four squares at a time with melted butter. Line the first tartlet tin with one square, gently easing it into the base and up the sides. Leave the edges overhanging.

5 Lay the remaining three buttered squares on top of the first, turning them so the corners form a star shape. Repeat for the remaining tartlet tins.

6 Beat the egg with the nutmeg and seasoning, then stir in the cheeses and spinach. Divide the mixture between the tins and level smooth. Fold the over-hanging pastry back over the filling.

7 Cut one of the remaining sheets of pastry into eight 10cm/4in rounds. Brush with butter and place two on top of each tartlet. Press around the edges to seal. Brush the remaining sheet of pastry with butter and cut into strips. Gently twist each strip and lay on top of the tartlets. Leave to stand for 5 minutes, then bake for about 30–35 minutes, until golden. Serve hot or cold.

Grilled Polenta with Peppers

INGREDIENTS

Serves 4

115g/4oz/scant 1 cup polenta
25g/1oz/2 tbsp butter
15–30ml/1–2 tbsp chopped mixed
 herbs, such as parsley, thyme
 and sage
melted butter, for brushing
60ml/4 tbsp olive oil
1–2 garlic cloves, cut into slivers
2 roasted red peppers, peeled and cut
 into strips
2 roasted yellow peppers, peeled and
 cut into strips
15ml/1 tbsp balsamic vinegar
salt and black pepper
fresh herb sprigs, to garnish

1 Bring 600ml/1 pint/2½ cups salted water to the boil in a heavy pan. Trickle in the polenta, beating continuously, then cook gently for 15–20 minutes, stirring occasionally, until the mixture is no longer grainy and comes away from the sides of the pan.

3 Pour the polenta into a small pudding basin, smooth the surface and leave until cold and firm.

2 Remove the pan from the heat and beat in the butter, herbs and plenty of freshly ground black pepper.

4 Turn out the polenta on to a board and cut into thick slices. Brush the polenta slices with melted butter and grill each side for about 4–5 minutes, until golden brown.

5 Meanwhile, heat the olive oil in a frying pan, add the garlic and peppers and stir-fry for 1–2 minutes. Stir in the balsamic vinegar and seasoning.

6 Spoon the pepper mixture over the polenta slices and garnish with fresh herb sprigs. Serve hot.

Chinese Vegetable Stir-fry

A typical stir-fried vegetable dish popular all over China. Chinese leaves are like a cross between a cabbage and a crunchy lettuce, with a delicious peppery flavour.

INGREDIENTS

Serves 4

45ml/3 tbsp sunflower oil
15ml/1 tbsp sesame oil
1 garlic clove, chopped
225g/8oz/2 cups broccoli florets, cut into small pieces
115g/4oz/1 cup sugar snap peas
1 whole Chinese leaf (about 450g/1lb) or Savoy cabbage, sliced
4 spring onions, finely chopped
30ml/2 tbsp soy sauce
30ml/2 tbsp dry sherry
15ml/1 tbsp sesame seeds, lightly toasted

1 Heat the oils in a wok or large frying pan until really hot, add the garlic and stir-fry for 30 seconds.

2 Add the broccoli florets and stir-fry for 3 minutes. Add the sugar snap peas and cook for 2 minutes, then tos in the Chinese leaves or cabbage and the spring onions and stir-fry for a further 2 minutes.

3 Pour on the soy sauce, sherry and 30–45ml/2–3 tbsp water and stir-fry for a further 4 minutes, or until the vegetables are just tender. Sprinkle with the toasted sesame seeds and serve hot.

Mixed Pepper Salad

INGREDIENTS

Serves 4

2 red peppers, halved and seeded
2 yellow peppers, halved and seeded
150ml/¼ pint/⅔ cup olive oil
1 onion, thinly sliced
2 garlic cloves, crushed
squeeze of lemon juice
chopped fresh parsley, to garnish

1 Grill the pepper halves for about 5 minutes, until the skin has blistered and blackened. Pop them into a polythene bag, seal and leave for 5 minutes.

2 Meanwhile, heat 30ml/2 tbsp of the olive oil in a frying pan and add the onion. Fry for about 5–6 minutes, until softened and translucent. Remove from the heat and reserve.

3 Take the peppers out of the bag and peel off the skins. Discard the pepper skins and slice each pepper half into fairly thin strips.

4 Place the peppers, cooked onions and any oil from the pan into a bowl. Add the crushed garlic and pour on the remaining olive oil, add a good squeeze of lemon juice and season. Mix well, cover and marinate for 2–3 hours, stirring the mixture once or twice.

5 Garnish the pepper salad with chopped fresh parsley and serve either as a tasty starter or as an accompaniment.

Thai Vegetables with Noodles

This dish makes a delicious vegetarian supper on its own, or serve it as an accompaniment.

INGREDIENTS

Serves 4
225g/8oz egg noodles
15ml/1 tbsp sesame oil
45ml/3 tbsp groundnut oil
2 garlic cloves, thinly sliced
2.5cm/1in piece fresh root ginger, finely chopped
2 fresh red chillies, seeded and sliced
115g/4oz broccoli, broken into small florets
115g/4oz baby corn cobs
175g/6oz shiitake or oyster mushrooms, sliced
1 bunch spring onions, sliced
115g/4oz bok choy or Chinese leaves, shredded
115g/4oz beansprouts
15–30ml/1–2 tbsp dark soy sauce
salt and black pepper

1 Cook the egg noodles in a pan of boiling salted water according to the packet instructions. Drain well and toss in the sesame oil. Set aside.

2 Heat the groundnut oil in a wok or large frying pan and stir-fry the garlic and ginger for 1 minute. Add the chillies, broccoli, corn cobs and mushrooms and stir-fry for a further 2 minutes.

3 Add the spring onions, shredded leaves and beansprouts and stir-fry for another 2 minutes.

4 Toss in the drained noodles with the soy sauce and ground black pepper.

5 Continue to cook over a high heat for a further 2–3 minutes, until the ingredients are well mixed and warmed through. Serve at once.

Swiss Soufflé Potatoes

Economical and satisfying, baked potatoes are great for cold-weather eating. Choose a floury variety of potato for the very best results.

INGREDIENTS

Serves 4
4 medium baking potatoes
115g/4oz Gruyère cheese, grated
115g/4oz/½ cup herb-flavoured butter
60ml/4 tbsp double cream
2 eggs, separated
salt and black pepper

1 Preheat the oven to 220°C/425°F/ Gas 7. Scrub the potatoes, then prick them all over with a fork. Bake for 1–1½ hours until tender. Remove them from the oven and reduce the temperature to 180°C/350°F/Gas 4.

2 Cut each potato in half and scoop out the flesh into a bowl. Return the potato shells to the oven to crisp them up while making the filling.

3 Mash the potato flesh using a fork, then add the Gruyère, herb-flavoured butter, cream, egg yolks and seasoning. Beat well until smooth.

4 Whisk the egg whites in a separate bowl until they hold stiff peaks, then fold into the potato mixture.

5 Pile the mixture back into the potato shells and bake for 20–25 minutes, until risen and golden brown.

Apple, Onion and Gruyère Tart

INGREDIENTS

Serves 4–6

225g/8oz/2 cups plain flour
1.25ml/¼ tsp dry mustard powder
75g/3oz/6 tbsp soft margarine
75g/3oz/6 tbsp Gruyère cheese, finely
  grated

For the filling

25g/1oz/2 tbsp butter
1 large onion, finely chopped
1 large or 2 small eating apples, peeled
  and grated
2 size 1 eggs
150ml/¼ pint/⅔ cup double cream
1.25ml/¼ tsp dried mixed herbs
2.5ml/½ tsp dry mustard powder
115g/4oz Gruyère cheese
salt and black pepper

1 To make the pastry, sift the flour, salt and mustard powder into a bowl. Rub in the margarine and cheese until the mixture forms soft bread-crumbs. Add 30ml/2 tbsp water and bring together into a ball. Chill, covered or wrapped, for 30 minutes.

2 Meanwhile, make the filling: melt the butter in a pan, add the onion and cook gently for 10 minutes, stirring occasionally, until softened but not browned. Stir in the apple and cook for 2–3 minutes. Leave to cool.

3 Roll out the pastry and line a light-ly greased 20cm/8in springform tin. Chill for 20 minutes. Preheat the oven to 200°C/400°F/Gas 6.

4 Line the pastry with greaseproof paper and fill with baking beans. Bake blind for 20 minutes.

5 Beat together the eggs, cream, herbs, seasoning and mustard. Grate three-quarters of the cheese and stir into the egg mixture, then slice the remaining cheese and set aside. When the pastry is cooked, remove the paper and beans and pour in the egg mixture.

6 Arrange the sliced cheese over the top. Reduce the oven temperature to 190°C/375°F/Gas 5. Return the tart to the oven and cook for a further 20 minutes, until the filling is golden and just firm. Serve hot or warm.

COOK'S TIP

You could substitute other hard cheeses, such as Cheddar, Lancashire, or Red Leicester for the Gruyère, if you prefer.

Golden Vegetable Paella

INGREDIENTS

Serves 4

pinch of saffron strands or 5ml/1 tsp
   ground turmeric
750ml/1¼ pints/3⅔ cups hot vegetable
   or spicy stock
90ml/6 tbsp olive oil
2 large onions, sliced
3 garlic cloves, chopped
275g/10oz/1⅓ cups long grain rice
50g/2oz/⅓ cup wild rice
175g/6oz pumpkin or butternut
   squash, chopped
175g/6oz carrots, cut in matchsticks
1 yellow pepper, seeded and sliced
4 tomatoes, peeled and chopped
115g/4oz oyster mushrooms, quartered
salt and black pepper
strips of red, yellow and green pepper,
   to garnish

1 Place the saffron in a small bowl with 45–60ml/3–4 tbsp boiling hot stock. Leave to stand for 5 minutes. Meanwhile, heat the oil in a paella pan or large heavy-based frying pan. Fry the onions and garlic gently until just softening.

2 Add the rices and toss for 2–3 minutes until coated in oil. Add the stock to the pan with the pumpkin or squash, and the saffron strands and liquid. Stir as it comes to the boil and reduce the heat to the minimum.

3 Cover with a pan lid or foil and cook very gently for about 15 minutes. (Avoid stirring unnecessarily as this lets out the steam and moistness.) Add the carrots, pepper, tomatoes, salt and black pepper, cover again and leave for a further 5 minutes, or until the rice is almost tender.

4 Finally, add the oyster mushrooms, check the seasoning and cook, uncovered, for just enough time to soften the mushrooms without letting the paella stick. Top with the peppers and serve as soon as possible.

Asparagus and Cheese Risotto

An authentic Italian risotto has a unique creamy texture achieved by constant stirring of the arborio rice, available from good supermarkets or delicatessens.

INGREDIENTS

Serves 4

1.25ml/¼ tsp saffron strands
750ml/1¼ pints/3⅔ cups hot vegetable stock
25g/1oz/2 tbsp butter
30ml/2 tbsp olive oil
1 large onion, finely chopped
2 garlic cloves, finely chopped
225g/8oz/1¼ cups arborio rice
300ml/½ pint/1¼ cups dry white wine
225g/8 oz asparagus tips (or asparagus cut into 5cm/2in lengths), cooked
75g/3oz/1 cup finely grated Parmesan cheese
salt and black pepper
Parmesan shavings and fresh basil sprigs, to garnish
ciabatta bread rolls and salad, to serve

1 Sprinkle the saffron over the stock and leave to stand for 5 minutes.

2 Heat the butter and oil in a frying pan, add the onions and garlic. Fry for about 6 minutes, until softened.

3 Add the rice and stir-fry for 1–2 minutes to coat the grains with the butter and oil.

4 Pour on 300ml/½ pint/1¼ cups of the hot vegetable stock and saffron. Cook gently over a moderate heat, stirring frequently, until all the liquid has been absorbed.

5 Repeat with another 300ml/½ pint/1¼ cups stock. When that has been absorbed, add the wine and carry on cooking and stirring until the rice has a creamy consistency.

6 Add the asparagus and remaining stock and stir until the liquid is absorbed and the rice is tender. Stir in the Parmesan cheese and season well.

7 Spoon the risotto on to warmed plates and garnish with the Parmesan cheese shavings and fresh basil. Serve with hot ciabatta rolls and a crisp green salad.

Goat's Cheese Salad

INGREDIENTS

Serves 4

30ml/2 tbsp olive oil
4 slices of French bread 1cm/½in thick
225g/8oz mixed salad leaves, such as
   curly endive, radicchio, and red oak
   leaf, torn in small pieces
4 firm goat's cheese rounds, about
   50g/2oz each, rind removed
1 yellow or red pepper, seeded and
   finely diced
1 small red onion, thinly sliced
45ml/3 tbsp chopped fresh parsley
30ml/2 tbsp snipped fresh chives

For the dressing

30ml/2 tbsp wine vinegar
5ml/1 tsp wholegrain mustard
75ml/5 tbsp olive oil
salt and black pepper

1 To make the dressing, mix the
vinegar and salt with a fork until
dissolved. Stir in the mustard.
Gradually stir in the oil until blended.
Season with pepper and set aside.
Preheat the grill.

2 Heat the oil in a frying pan.
When hot, add the bread slices
and cook for 1 minute until golden.
Turn and cook the other side for
about 30 seconds more. Drain on
kitchen paper and set aside.

3 Place the salad leaves in a bowl.
Add 45ml/3 tbsp of the dressing
and toss to coat. Divide the dressed
leaves among four salad plates.

4 Put the goat's cheeses, cut side up,
on a baking sheet and grill for 1–2
minutes until bubbling and golden.

5 Set one goat's cheese on each slice
of bread and place in the centre
of each plate. Scatter the diced pepper,
red onion, parsley, and chives over the
salad. Drizzle with the remaining dressing and serve.

VARIATION

For a more substantial main course salad,
increase the amount of salad leaves and
make double the quantity of dressing. Add
115g/4oz sliced cooked green beans to the
leaves, and toss with half of the dressing.
Top with the goat's cheeses and remaining
dressing.

Creamy Potato Gratin with Herbs

INGREDIENTS

Serves 4

675g/1½lb waxy potatoes
25g/1oz/2 tbsp butter
1 onion, finely chopped
1 garlic clove, crushed
2 eggs
300ml/½ pint/1¼ cups crème fraîche
    or double cream
115g/4oz Gruyère cheese, grated
60ml/4 tbsp chopped fresh mixed
    herbs, such as chervil, thyme, chives
    and parsley
freshly grated nutmeg
salt and black pepper

1 Place a baking sheet in the oven and preheat to 190°C/375°F/Gas 5.

2 Peel the potatoes and cut into matchsticks. Set aside. Melt the butter in a pan and fry the onion and garlic until softened. In a large bowl whisk together the eggs, crème fraîche or cream and half of the cheese.

3 Stir in the onion mixture, herbs, potatoes, salt, pepper and nutmeg. Spoon into a buttered ovenproof dish and sprinkle over the remaining cheese. Bake on the hot baking sheet for 50–60 minutes, until golden brown.

Spinach Roulade with Mushrooms

INGREDIENTS

Serves 6–8

450g/1lb fresh spinach
15g/½oz/1 tbsp butter
4 eggs, separated
freshly grated nutmeg
50g/2oz Cheddar cheese, grated
salt and black pepper

For the filling

25g/1oz/2 tbsp butter
350g/12oz button mushrooms,
    chopped
25g/1oz/¼ cup plain flour
150ml/¼ pint/⅔ cup milk
45ml/3 tbsp double cream
30ml/2 tbsp snipped fresh chives

1 Preheat the oven to 190°C/375°F/ Gas 5. Line a 23 x 33cm/ 9 x 13in Swiss roll tin with non-stick baking paper. Wash the spinach and remove the stalks, then cook the wet leaves in a covered pan without extra water until just tender. Drain the spinach well, squeeze out all the excess moisture and then chop finely.

2 Tip the spinach into a bowl, beat in the butter and egg yolks and season with salt, pepper and nutmeg. Whisk the egg whites until stiff and fold into the spinach mixture. Spread into the tin and sprinkle with half the cheese. Bake for 10–12 minutes, until just firm.

3 Meanwhile, make the filling. Melt the butter in a pan and fry the mushrooms until tender, stir in the flour and cook for 1 minute. Gradually add the milk, then bring to the boil, stirring until thickened. Simmer for a further 2–3 minutes. Remove from the heat and stir in the cream and chives.

4 Remove the cooked roulade from the oven and turn out on to a sheet of non-stick baking paper. Peel off the lining paper and spread the roulade evenly with the mushroom filling.

5 Roll up the roulade fairly tightly and transfer to an ovenproof dish. Sprinkle over the remaining cheese and return the roulade to the oven for about 4–5 minutes to melt the cheese. Serve at once, cut into slices.

Baby Leaf Salad with Croûtons

INGREDIENTS

Serves 4

15ml/1 tbsp olive oil
1 garlic clove, crushed
15ml/1 tbsp freshly grated Parmesan
   cheese
15ml/1 tbsp chopped fresh parsley
4 slices ciabatta bread, crusts removed,
   cut into small cubes
1 large bunch watercress
large handful of rocket
1 bag mixed baby salad leaves, including oak leaf and cos lettuce
1 ripe avocado

For the dressing

45ml/3 tbsp olive oil
15ml/1 tbsp walnut oil
juice of ½ lemon
2.5ml/½ tsp Dijon mustard
salt and black pepper

1 Preheat the oven to 190°C/375°F/ Gas 5. Put the oil, garlic, Parmesan, parsley and bread in a bowl and toss to coat well. Spread out the bread cubes on a baking sheet and bake for about 8 minutes until crisp. Leave to cool.

2 Remove any coarse or discoloured stalks or leaves from the watercress and place in a serving bowl with the rocket and baby salad leaves.

3 Halve the avocado and remove the stone. Peel and cut into chunks, then add it to the salad bowl.

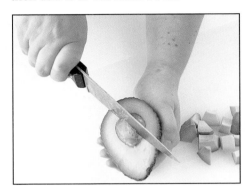

4 To make the dressing, mix together the oils, lemon juice, mustard and seasoning in a small bowl or screw-topped jar until evenly blended. Pour over the salad and toss well. Sprinkle over the croûtons and serve at once.

Wild Rice with Grilled Vegetables

Grilling brings out the flavour of these summer vegetables.

INGREDIENTS

Serves 4

115g/4oz/⅔ cup wild rice
115g/4oz/⅔ cup long-grain white rice
1 large aubergine, thickly sliced
1 red, 1 yellow and 1 green pepper,
   seeded and cut into quarters
2 red onions, sliced
225g/8oz brown cap or shiitake
   mushrooms
2 small courgettes, cut in half
   lengthways
olive oil, for brushing
30ml/2 tbsp chopped fresh thyme

For the dressing

90ml/6 tbsp extra virgin olive oil
30ml/2 tbsp balsamic vinegar
2 garlic cloves, crushed
salt and black pepper

1 Put the wild rice in a pan of cold salted water. Bring to the boil, then reduce the heat, cover and cook gently for 25 minutes before adding the white rice. Cook for a further 10 minutes, or until the grains are tender.

2 To make the dressing, mix together the olive oil, vinegar, garlic and seasoning in a bowl or screw-topped jar until well blended. Set aside while you grill the vegetables.

3 Arrange the vegetables on a grill rack. Brush with olive oil and grill for 8–10 minutes, until tender and well browned, turning them occasionally and brushing again with oil.

4 Drain the rice and toss in half the dressing. Tip into a serving dish and arrange the grilled vegetables on top. Pour over the remaining dressing and scatter over the chopped thyme.

Potato and Red Pepper Frittata

Fresh herbs make all the difference in this simple but delicious recipe – parsley or chives could be substituted for the chopped mint.

Ingredients

Serves 3–4

450g/1lb small new potatoes
6 eggs
30ml/2 tbsp chopped fresh mint
30ml/2 tbsp olive oil
1 onion, chopped
2 garlic cloves, crushed
2 red peppers, seeded and roughly chopped
salt and black pepper
mint sprigs, to garnish

1 Scrub the potatoes, then cook in a pan of boiling salted water until just tender. Drain the potatoes, leave to cool slightly, then cut into thick slices.

2 Whisk together the eggs, mint and seasoning in a bowl, then set aside. Heat the oil in a large frying pan.

3 Add the onion, garlic, peppers and potatoes to the pan and cook, stirring, for 5 minutes.

4 Pour the egg mixture over the vegetables and stir gently.

5 Push the mixture into the centre of the pan as it cooks to allow the liquid egg to run on to the base.

6 Once the egg mixture is lightly set, place the pan under a hot grill for 2–3 minutes, until golden brown. Serve hot or cold, cut into wedges and garnished with sprigs of mint.

Red Onion Galettes

Red onions have a wonderful mild flavour – don't be tempted to substitute Spanish-style onions.

INGREDIENTS

Serves 4

60–75ml/4–5 tbsp olive oil
500g/1¼lb red onions, sliced
1 garlic clove, crushed
30ml/2 tbsp chopped fresh mixed
  herbs, such as thyme, parsley
  and basil
225g/8oz ready-made puff pastry
15ml/1 tbsp sun-dried tomato paste
black pepper
thyme sprigs, to garnish

1 Heat 30ml/2 tbsp of the oil in a pan and add the onions and garlic. Cover and cook gently for 15–20 minutes, stirring occasionally, until soft but not browned. Stir in the herbs.

2 Preheat the oven to 220°C/425°F/ Gas 7. Divide the pastry into four equal pieces and roll out each one to a 15cm/6in round. Flute the edges and prick all over with a fork. Place on baking sheets and chill for 10 minutes.

3 Mix 15ml/1 tbsp of the remaining olive oil with the sun-dried tomato paste and brush over the centres of the rounds, leaving a 1cm/½in border.

4 Spread the onion mixture over the pastry rounds and grind over plenty of pepper. Drizzle over a little more oil, then bake for about 15 minutes, until the pastry is crisp and golden. Serve hot, garnished with thyme sprigs.

Twice-baked Cheddar Soufflés

This is an ace of a recipe for busy people and really easy to make. The soufflés can be prepared well in advance, then simply reheated just before serving.

INGREDIENTS

Serves 4

300ml/½ pint/1¼ cups milk
flavouring ingredients (a few onion slices, 1 bay leaf and 4 black peppercorns)
65g/2½oz/5 tbsp butter
40g/1½oz/⅓ cup plain flour
115g/4oz mature Cheddar cheese, grated
1.25ml/¼ tsp mustard powder
3 eggs, separated
20ml/4 tsp chopped fresh parsley
250ml/8fl oz/1 cup double cream
salt and black pepper

1 Preheat the oven to 180°C/350°F/ Gas 4. Put the milk in a pan with the flavouring ingredients. Bring slowly to the boil, then strain into a jug.

— COOK'S TIP —

Don't attempt to unmould the soufflés until they have cooled, when they will be firmer and easier to handle. They can be kept chilled for up to 8 hours. Use snipped fresh chives instead of the parsley, if you like.

---

2 Melt the butter in the rinsed-out pan and use a little to grease four 150ml/¼ pint/⅔ cup ramekins.

3 Stir the flour into the remaining butter in the pan and cook for 1 minute. Gradually add the hot milk, then bring to the boil, stirring until thickened and smooth. Cook, stirring all the time, for 2 minutes.

4 Remove the pan from the heat and stir in 75g/3oz of the grated cheese and the mustard powder. Beat in the egg yolks, followed by the chopped parsley, and season to taste with salt and black pepper.

5 Whisk the egg whites in a large bowl until stiff but not dry. Mix in a spoonful of the egg whites to lighten the cheese mixture, then gently fold in the remaining egg whites.

6 Spoon the soufflé mixture into the ramekins, place in a roasting tin and pour in boiling water to come halfway up the sides. Bake the soufflés for 15–20 minutes until risen and set. Remove the ramekins immediately from the tin and allow the soufflés to sink and cool, until ready to serve.

7 When ready to serve, preheat the oven to 220°C/ 425°F/Gas 7. Carefully turn out the soufflés into a buttered shallow ovenproof dish or individual dishes. Season the cream and pour over the soufflés, then sprinkle over the remaining cheese.

8 Bake the soufflés for about 10–15 minutes, until risen and golden brown. Serve at once.

Pear and Roquefort Salad

Choose ripe, firm Comice or Williams' pears for this salad.

INGREDIENTS

Serves 4
3 ripe pears
lemon juice
about 175g/6oz mixed salad leaves
175g/6oz Roquefort cheese
50g/2oz/½ cup hazelnut kernels, toasted and chopped

For the dressing
30ml/2 tbsp hazelnut oil
45ml/3 tbsp olive oil
15ml/1 tbsp cider vinegar
5ml/1 tsp Dijon mustard
salt and black pepper

1 To make the dressing, mix together the oils, vinegar and mustard in a bowl or screw-topped jar. Add salt and black pepper to taste.

2 Peel, core and slice the pears and toss them in lemon juice.

3 Arrange the salad leaves on serving plates, then arrange the pears on top. Crumble the Roquefort cheese and scatter over the salad with the chopped, toasted hazelnuts. Serve at once.

Onion and Gruyère Tart

The secret of this tart is to cook the onions very slowly until they almost caramelize.

INGREDIENTS

Serves 4
175g/6oz/1½ cups plain flour
pinch of salt
75g/3oz/6 tbsp butter, diced
1 egg yolk

For the filling
50g/2oz/4 tbsp butter
450g/1lb onions, thinly sliced
15–30ml/1–2 tbsp wholegrain mustard
2 eggs, plus 1 egg yolk
300ml/½ pint/1 cup double cream
75g/3oz Gruyère cheese, grated
freshly grated nutmeg
salt and black pepper

1 To make the pastry, sift the flour and salt into a bowl, then rub in the butter until the mixture resembles fine breadcrumbs. Add the egg yolk and 15ml/1 tbsp cold water and mix to a firm dough. Chill for 30 minutes.

2 Preheat the oven to 200°C/400°F/ Gas 6. Knead the pastry, then roll out on a floured board and use to line a 23cm/9in flan tin. Prick the base with a fork, line the pastry case with grease-proof paper and fill with baking beans.

3 Bake the pastry case for 15 minutes. Remove the paper and beans and bake for a further 10–15 minutes, until the pastry case is crisp. Meanwhile, melt the butter and cook the onions in a covered pan for 20 minutes, stirring occasionally, until golden.

4 Reduce the oven temperature to 180°C/350°F/Gas 4. Spread the base with mustard and top with the onions. Mix together the eggs, egg yolk, cream, cheese, nutmeg and seasoning. Pour over the onions. Bake for 30–35 minutes, until golden. Serve warm.

SIDE DISHES & SALADS

These delicious dishes make enticing and interesting accompaniments to all sorts of vegetarian main courses. There are recipes for all through the year – Bombay Spiced Potatoes, Parsnips with Almonds, or Baked Courgettes in Passata are perfect for chilly days. While in the summer you might like to try the colourful Spinach and Beetroot Salad or Parcels of Baked Baby Vegetables.

Parsnips with Almonds

Parsnips have an affinity with most nuts, so you could substitute walnuts or hazelnuts for the almonds.

INGREDIENTS

Serves 4
450g/1lb small parsnips
35g/1¼ oz/scant 3 tbsp butter
25g/1oz/¼ cup flaked almonds
15ml/1 tbsp soft light brown sugar
pinch of mixed spice
15ml/1 tbsp lemon juice
salt and black pepper
chopped fresh chervil or parsley,
  to garnish

1 Cook the parsnips in boiling salted water until almost tender. Drain well. When the parsnips are cool enough to handle, cut each in half across its width. Quarter the wide halves lengthways.

2 Heat the butter in a frying pan. Add the parsnips and almonds and cook gently, stirring and turning the parsnips carefully until they are lightly flecked with brown.

3 Mix together the sugar and mixed spice, sprinkle over the parsnips and stir to mix, then trickle over the lemon juice. Season and heat for 1 minute. Serve sprinkled with chopped fresh chervil or parsley.

COOK'S TIP

You could replace the mixed spice with Chinese five spice powder, if you prefer.

Turnips with Orange

Sprinkle toasted nuts such as flaked almonds or chopped walnuts or hazelnuts over the turnips to add a contrasting texture and taste.

INGREDIENTS

Serves 4
50g/2oz/4 tbsp butter
15ml/1 tbsp oil
1 small shallot, finely chopped
450g/1lb small turnips, quartered
300ml/½ pint/1¼ cups freshly
  squeezed orange juice
salt and black pepper

1 Heat the butter and oil in a saucepan, then cook the shallot gently, stirring occasionally, until soft but not coloured.

2 Add the turnips to the shallot and heat, shaking the pan frequently, until the turnips seem to be absorbing the butter and oil.

3 Pour the orange juice on to the turnips, then simmer gently for about 30 minutes, until the turnips are tender and the orange juice reduced to a buttery sauce.

COOK'S TIP

You could add some spice such as ground ginger, cinnamon or crushed cumin seeds.

Rosemary Roasties

These unusual roast potatoes use far less fat than traditional roast potatoes, and because they still have their skins they not only absorb less oil but have more flavour too.

INGREDIENTS 🍎

Serves 4
900g/2lb small red potatoes
10ml/2 tsp walnut or sunflower oil
30ml/2 tbsp fresh rosemary leaves
salt and paprika

1 Preheat the oven to 225°C/475°F/ Gas 7. Leave the potatoes whole with the peel on, or if large, cut in half. Place the potatoes in a large pan of cold water and bring to the boil. Drain well.

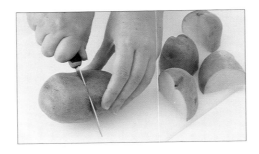

2 Drizzle the walnut or sunflower oil over the potatoes and shake the pan to coat them evenly.

3 Tip the potatoes into a shallow roasting pan. Sprinkle with rosemary, salt and paprika. Roast for 30 minutes or until crisp. Serve hot.

VARIATION

To make Nutty Rosemary Roasties, scatter over a handful of chopped hazelnuts, walnuts or almonds about 5 minutes before the end of cooking.

Baked Courgettes in Passata

INGREDIENTS

Serves 4
5ml/1 tsp olive oil
3 large courgettes, thinly sliced
½ small red onion, finely chopped
300ml/½ pint/¼ cups passata
30ml/2 tbsp chopped fresh thyme
garlic salt and black pepper
fresh thyme sprigs, to garnish

1 Preheat the oven to 190°C/375°F/ Gas 5. Brush an ovenproof dish with olive oil. Arrange half the courgettes and onion in the dish.

2 Spoon half the passata over the vegetables and sprinkle with some of the fresh thyme, then season to taste with garlic salt and pepper.

3 Arrange the remaining courgettes and onion in the dish on top of the sauce, then season to taste with more garlic salt and pepper. Spoon over the remaining sauce and spread evenly.

4 Cover the dish with foil, then bake for 40–45 minutes, or until the courgettes are tender. Garnish with sprigs of thyme and serve hot.

COOK'S TIP

Red onions have a lovely mild taste, but if you don't have one, then just use half an ordinary onion instead, or if you find them, substitute one or two shallots which also have a mild flavour.

Parcels of Baked Baby Vegetables

If baby vegetables are unavailable use larger vegetables cut into bite-sized pieces.

INGREDIENTS

Serves 2

50g/2oz/4 tbsp unsalted butter
30ml/2 tbsp chopped fresh mixed herbs
1 garlic clove
2.5ml/½ tsp grated lemon rind
30ml/2 tbsp olive oil
350–450g/12oz–1lb mixed baby
   vegetables, such as carrots, turnips,
   parsnips, fennel and patty-pan squash
6 baby onions, peeled
lemon juice (optional)
salt and black pepper
shavings of Pecorino or Parmesan
   cheese or soft goat's cheese, and
   crusty bread, to serve

1 Preheat the oven to 220°C/425°F/ Gas 7. Put the butter, herbs, garlic and lemon rind in a food processor and process until blended. Season to taste.

2 Heat the oil in a frying pan or wok and stir-fry the vegetables for about 3 minutes, until lightly browned.

3 Divide the vegetables equally between two sheets of foil and dot with the herb butter. Close the parcels tightly and place on a baking sheet. Bake for 30–40 minutes, until just tender.

4 Carefully unwrap the parcels and add a squeeze of lemon juice, if needed, to perk up the flavours.

5 Serve the vegetables in the parcels or transfer to warmed soup plates. Spoon over the juices and accompany with the cheese and crusty bread.

Watercress and Potato Salad

New potatoes are equally good hot or cold, and this colourful, nutritious salad is an ideal way of making the most of them.

INGREDIENTS 🍎

Serves 4

450g/1lb small new potatoes, unpeeled
1 bunch watercress
200g/7oz/1½ cups cherry tomatoes, halved
30ml/2 tbsp pumpkin seeds
45ml/3 tbsp low fat fromage frais
15ml/1 tbsp cider vinegar
5ml/1 tsp brown sugar
salt and paprika

1 Cook the potatoes in lightly salted, boiling water until just tender, then drain and leave to cool.

2 Toss together the potatoes, watercress, tomatoes, and pumpkin seeds.

3 Place the fromage frais, vinegar, sugar, salt, and paprika in a screw-top jar and shake well to mix. Pour over the salad just before serving.

— VARIATION —

To make Spinach and Potato Salad, substitute about 225g/8oz fresh baby spinach leaves for the watercress.

— COOK'S TIP —

If you are preparing this salad in advance, mix the dressing in the jar and toss in just before serving.

Bombay Spiced Potatoes

This Indian potato dish uses a mixture of whole and ground spices. Look out for mustard and black onion seeds in specialist food shops.

INGREDIENTS

Serves 4

4 large potatoes (Maris Piper or King Edward), cubed
60ml/4 tbsp sunflower oil
1 garlic clove, finely chopped
10ml/2 tsp brown mustard seeds
5ml/1 tsp black onion seeds (optional)
5ml/1 tsp ground turmeric
5ml/1 tsp ground cumin
5ml/1 tsp ground coriander
5ml/1 tsp fennel seeds
salt and black pepper
a good squeeze of lemon juice
chopped fresh coriander and lemon wedges, to garnish

1 Bring a pan of salted water to the boil, add the potatoes and simmer for about 4 minutes, until just tender. Drain well.

2 Heat the oil in a large frying pan and add the garlic along with all the whole and ground spices. Fry gently for 1–2 minutes, stirring until the mustard seeds start to pop.

3 Add the potatoes and stir-fry on a moderate heat for about 5 minutes, until heated through and well coated with the spicy oil.

4 Season well and sprinkle over the lemon juice. Garnish with chopped coriander and lemon wedges. Serve as an accompaniment to curries or other strong flavoured dishes.

Spanish Chilli Potatoes

The name of this Spanish *tapas* dish, *Patatas Bravas*, means fierce, hot potatoes. You can always reduce the amount of chilli to suit your taste.

INGREDIENTS

Serves 4

1kg/2lb new or salad potatoes
60ml/4 tbsp olive oil
1 onion, finely chopped
2 garlic cloves, crushed
15ml/1 tbsp tomato purée
200g/7oz can chopped tomatoes
15ml/1 tbsp red wine vinegar
2–3 small dried red chillies, seeded and chopped finely, or 5–10ml/1–2 tsp hot chilli powder
5ml/1 tsp paprika
salt and black pepper
fresh flat leaf parsley sprig, to garnish

1 Boil the potatoes in their skins for 10–12 minutes or until just tender. Drain well and leave to cool, then cut in half and reserve.

2 Heat the oil in a large pan and add the onions and garlic. Fry gently for 5–6 minutes, until just softened. Stir in the tomato purée, tomatoes, vinegar, chilli and paprika and simmer for about 5 minutes.

3 Add the potatoes and mix into the sauce mixture until well coated. Cover and simmer gently for about 8–10 minutes, or until the potatoes are tender. Season well and transfer to a warmed serving dish. Serve garnished with a sprig of flat leaf parsley.

Chinese Crispy Seaweed

In northern China they use a special kind of seaweed for this dish, but spring greens, shredded very finely, make a very good alternative. Serve either as a starter or as an accompaniment to a Chinese meal.

INGREDIENTS

Serves 4
225g/8oz spring greens
groundnut or corn oil, for deep-frying
1.25ml/½ tsp salt
10ml/2 tsp soft light brown sugar
30–45ml/2–3 tbsp toasted, flaked
  almonds

1 Cut out and discard any tough stalks from the spring greens. Place about six leaves on top of each other and roll up into a tight roll.

2 Using a sharp knife, slice across into thin shreds. Lay on a tray and leave to dry for about 2 hours.

3 Heat about 5–7.5cm/2–3in of oil in a wok or pan to 190°C/375°F. Carefully place a handful of the leaves into the oil – it will bubble and spit for the first 10 seconds and then die down. Deep-fry for about 45 seconds, or until a slightly darker green – do not to let the leaves burn.

4 Remove with a slotted spoon, drain on kitchen paper and transfer to a serving dish. Keep warm in the oven while frying the remainder.

5 When you have fried all the shredded leaves, sprinkle with the salt and sugar and toss lightly. Garnish with the toasted almonds.

> —————— COOK'S TIP ——————
>
> Make sure that your deep-frying pan is deep enough to allow the oil to bubble up during cooking. The pan should be less than half full.

Leek and Parsnip Purée

Vegetable purées are delicious served as an accompaniment to a vegetarian main course. This mixture of leeks and parsnips is especially good.

INGREDIENTS

Serves 4
2 large leeks, sliced
3 medium parsnips, sliced
knob of butter
45ml/3 tbsp top of the milk
30ml/2 tbsp fromage frais
a good squeeze of lemon juice
salt and black pepper
a good pinch of grated nutmeg to
  garnish

1 Steam or boil the leeks and parsnips together for about 15 minutes, until tender. Drain well, then place in a food processor or blender.

2 Add the remaining ingredients to the processor or blender. Whizz until really smooth, then check the seasoning. Transfer to a warmed bowl and garnish with a sprinkling of nutmeg.

Garlic Baked Tomatoes

If you can find them, use Italian plum tomatoes, which have a warm, slightly sweet flavour. For large numbers of people you could use the very tiny tomatoes, not halved but tossed several times during cooking.

INGREDIENTS

Serves 4
40g/1½oz/3 tbsp unsalted butter
1 large garlic clove, crushed
5ml/1 tsp finely grated orange rind
4 firm plum tomatoes, or 2 large beef
 tomatoes
salt and black pepper
shredded basil leaves, to garnish

1 Soften the butter and blend with the crushed garlic, orange rind, and seasoning. Chill for a few minutes.

2 Preheat the oven to 200°C/400°F/ Gas 6. Halve the tomatoes cross-ways and trim the bases so they stand.

3 Place the tomatoes in an oven-proof dish and spread the butter equally over each tomato half.

4 Bake the tomatoes in the oven for 15–25 minutes, depending on the size of the tomato halves, until just tender. Serve sprinkled with the basil.

--- FREEZER NOTE ---

Garlic butter is well worth keeping in the freezer. Make it up as above, or omit the orange rind and add chopped fresh parsley. Freeze in thick slices or chunks ready to use, or roll into a sausage shape and wrap in foil, then cut into slices when partly defrosted.

Lemon Carrot Salad

You don't need to be on a diet to enjoy this tangy, colourful and refreshing salad.

INGREDIENTS

Serves 4–6
450g/1lb small, young carrots
grated rind and juice of ½ lemon
15ml/1 tbsp soft light brown sugar
60ml/4 tbsp sunflower oil
5ml/1 tsp hazelnut or sesame oil
5ml/1 tsp chopped fresh oregano,
 or pinch of dried
salt and black pepper

1 Finely grate the carrots and place them in a large bowl. Stir in the lemon rind, 15–30ml/1–2 tbsp of the lemon juice, the sugar, sunflower and hazelnut or sesame oils, and mix well.

2 Add more lemon juice and season-ing to taste, then sprinkle on the oregano, toss lightly and leave the salad for 1 hour before serving.

--- COOK'S TIP ---

Other root vegetables could be used in this salad. For instance, you could try replacing half the carrot with swede, or use celeriac or kohlrabi instead.

Chinese Sprouts

If you are bored with plain boiled Brussels sprouts, try pepping them up with this unusual stir-fried method, which uses the minimum of oil.

INGREDIENTS 🍎

Serves 4
450g/1lb Brussels sprouts, shredded
5ml/1 tsp sesame or sunflower oil
2 spring onions, sliced
2.5ml/½ tsp Chinese five-spice powder
15ml/1 tbsp light soy sauce

1 Trim the Brussels sprouts, then shred them finely using a large sharp knife or shred in a food processor.

2 Heat the oil and add the sprouts and onions, then stir-fry for about 2 minutes, without browning.

3 Stir in the five-spice powder and soy sauce, then cook, stirring, for 2–3 minutes more, until just tender.

4 Serve hot, other vegetarian Chinese dishes.

COOK'S TIP

Brussels sprouts are rich in Vitamin C, and this is a good way to cook them to preserve the vitamins. Larger sprouts cook particularly well by this method, and cabbage can also be cooked this way.

Cracked Wheat and Fennel

INGREDIENTS

Serves 4

115g/4oz/¾ cup cracked wheat
1 large fennel bulb, finely chopped
115g/4oz green beans, chopped and
  blanched
1 small orange
1 garlic clove, crushed
30–45ml/2–3 tbsp sunflower oil
15ml/1 tbsp white wine vinegar
salt and black pepper
½ red or orange pepper, seeded and
  finely chopped, to garnish

1 Place the wheat in a bowl and cover with boiling water. Leave for 10–15 minutes, stirring occasionally. When doubled in size, drain well and squeeze out any excess water.

2 While still slightly warm, stir in the chopped fennel and the green beans. Finely grate the orange rind into a bowl. Peel and segment the orange and stir into the salad.

3 Add the crushed garlic to the orange rind, then add the sunflower oil, white wine vinegar, and seasoning to taste, and mix thoroughly. Pour this dressing over the salad, mix well. Chill the salad for 1–2 hours.

4 Serve the salad sprinkled with the chopped red or orange pepper.

Beans with Tomatoes

Young runner beans should not have 'strings' down the sides, but older ones will and they should be removed before cooking.

INGREDIENTS

Serves 4

675g/1½lb runner beans, sliced
40g/1½oz/3 tbsp butter
4 ripe tomatoes, peeled and chopped
salt and black pepper
chopped fresh tarragon, to garnish

COOK'S TIP

French beans can be used instead of runner beans, but reduce the cooking time slightly.

1 Add the beans to a saucepan of boiling water, return to the boil, then boil for 3 minutes. Drain well.

2 Heat the butter in a saucepan and add the tomatoes, beans and seasoning. Cover the pan and simmer gently for 10–15 minutes, until the beans are tender.

3 Tip the beans and tomatoes into a warm serving dish and sprinkle over the chopped tarragon. Serve hot as an accompaniment.

Spinach and Beetroot Salad

INGREDIENTS

Serves 4–6

45ml/3 tbsp light olive oil
5–6.25ml/1–1¼ tsp caraway seeds
juice of 1 orange
5ml/1 tsp caster sugar
675g/1½lb cooked beetroot, diced
salt and black pepper
young spinach leaves, to serve
chopped fresh parsley, to garnish

1 Arrange the spinach leaves in a shallow salad bowl.

2 Heat the oil in a saucepan, add the caraway seeds, orange juice, sugar and salt and pepper.

3 Add the beetroot and shake the pan to coat it with the dressing.

4 Spoon the warm beetroot and dressing mixture in amongst the spinach and sprinkle with the chopped parsley. Serve at once either as an accompaniment or as a main course.

COOK'S TIP

Use freshly cooked beetroot, not those that have been steeped in vinegar.

New Potato Parcels

Even with the oven packed full, you should still be able to find a corner for these delicious potatoes. If necessary, cook them in individual portions. They could be put over a barbecue or real fire, too, and left for long slow cooking.

INGREDIENTS

Serves 4
16–20 very small potatoes in their skins
60ml/4 tbsp olive oil
1–2 sprigs each of thyme, tarragon and oregano, or 15ml/1 tbsp mixed dried herbs
salt and black pepper

1 Preheat the oven to 200°C/400°F/ Gas 6. Grease one large sheet or four small sheets of foil.

2 Put the potatoes in a large bowl and add in the rest of the ingredients and seasonings. Mix well so the potatoes are thoroughly coated.

3 Put the potatoes into the middle of the foil and seal up the parcel(s). Place on a baking sheet and bake for 40–50 minutes. The potatoes will stay warm for quite some time.

Stir-fried Florets with Hazelnuts

A rich hazelnut dressing turns crunchy cauliflower and broccoli into a very special vegetable dish.

INGREDIENTS

Serves 4
175g/6oz/1½ cups cauliflower florets
175g/6oz/1½ cups broccoli florets
15ml/1 tbsp sunflower oil
50g/2oz/½ cup hazelnuts, finely chopped
¼ red chilli, finely chopped, or 5ml/ 1 tsp chilli powder (optional)
60ml/4 tbsp crème fraîche or fromage frais
salt and black pepper
thin rings of chilli or chopped red pepper, to garnish

1 Make sure the cauliflower and broccoli florets are all of an even size. Heat the oil in a saucepan or wok and toss the florets over a high heat for 1 minute.

2 Reduce the heat and continue stir-frying for another 5 minutes, then add the hazelnuts, chilli and seasoning.

3 When the cauliflower is crisp and nearly tender, stir in the crème fraîche or fromage frais and just heat through. Serve at once, sprinkled with the chilli rings or chopped pepper.

COOK'S TIP

The crisper these florets are the better, so cook them just long enough to make them piping hot, and give them time to absorb all the flavours.

INDEX